Third Age Press

ISBN 978-1-898576-40-8
First edition

Third Age Press Ltd, 2009
Third Age Press, 6 Parkside Gardens
London SW19 5EY
Managing Editor Dianne Norton

Photographs and playbills
from the Patrick Newley collection

Drawings by Clarke Hutton taken from *Byng Ballads* (1932)
and *More Byng Ballads* (1935) published by John Lane ,
The Bodley Head

Cover & layout design by Dianne Norton
Printed and bound in Great Britain
by IntypeLibra London

BAWDY BUT BRITISH!

THE LIFE OF DOUGLAS BYNG

by

PATRICK NEWLEY

ABOUT THE AUTHOR

PATRICK NEWLEY is a longstanding
contributor to both *The Times* and *The Stage*
newspapers. He has also written for *The
Daily Express* and many other publications. A
frequent broadcaster for the BBC, he was press
agent for the writers Quentin Crisp and Robin
Maugham. He managed the later careers of both
the legendary revue artiste Douglas Byng and
the comedian Rex Jameson (Mrs Shufflewick).
His publications for Third Age Press include
*The Amazing Mrs Shufflewick: The Life of Rex
Jameson* (2007),and *You Lucky People! The
Tommy Trinder Story (2008)*. Patrick lives in
London.

FOR ANDREW VISNEVSKI

Just to introduce myself –
I'm Douglas Byng, I entertained at supper,
The smarter members of the class called upper.
Those idle rich who never went to bed
And clamoured for amusement while they fed
Where debutantes acquired the champagne habit
In evening wraps of ermine or white rabbit
And actresses with tempers and mink sables
Raised hell because they hadn't booked a table.

My songs are said to be a trifle risqué
And made the nicest dowagers so frisky.
Sedate jet black bosoms heaved with laughter,
Their daughters pointed jokes out to them after.
And though the tone of Mendelsohnn's own Spring
Song
May perhaps be more artistic than a Byng song
I still maintain I've nothing to feel shy about,
I told the young those things their parents lie about . . .

CONTENTS

ILLUSTRATIONS

INTRODUCTION

Douglas Byng was one of the British theatre's great stage stars, an actor who, like many of his contemporaries including Rex Harrison, Noel Coward, Robert Morley and Stanley Holloway, earned much of their living performing on the London stage. They topped bills and often enjoyed record-breaking long runs, were warmly welcomed on stage to rounds of applause, had their own specially designed entrances and exits within a production, and, rarely, if ever, missed a performance. After a show there was always a big crowd of fans waiting for them outside the stage door and these great performers did not disappoint.

Stage stars in Britain today no longer exist. They have no place in today's ensemble or director orientated theatre and therefore are an extinct race.

Douglas Byng's career as a stage star lasted almost an astonishing seventy years, a record unbeaten, so far, by any British actor. Born in 1893 he made his first professional appearance in 1914 as the lead comedian in a concert party and by 1921 was appearing at the London Palladium. In 1987, shortly before his death, he was performing his one-man show to a packed audience at the National Theatre.

But Byng's career was notable not just for its longevity but for its originality. He was a prolific songwriter, often writing highly risqué material for the period. He was banned by the BBC several times and, during World War Two, was once, somewhat incredibly, thought 'too blue for the troops'.

He was also an accomplished costume designer, a brilliantly funny and glamorous pantomime dame and, above all, a supreme cabaret artiste who appeared in some of the world's top nightclubs. More than this, his act, performed when homosexuality was illegal in Britain, was outrageously camp, so much so, he was dubbed the 'high priest' of the genre.

He didn't enjoy the sobriquet and rarely talked about his own homosexuality. He was a private man and felt that his personal life had nothing to do with the stage but for thousands of gay men during the 1920s and long after, he was something of a gay icon.

Dougie – as he was affectionately known by his friends and theatregoers – often mentally divided his audiences into two. In pantomime there were jokes for the children and jokes for the adults. Inevitably, the kids laughed at the adult jokes and vice versa. In cabaret the 1920s dowager duchesses and society hostesses laughed at what they thought was obviously 'naughty' material – but gays in the audience were quick to spot the innuendo.

As a female impersonator, both in pantomime, revue and cabaret, Dougie paved the way for the likes of future stars such as Danny La Rue – La Rue has said that much of his career has been inspired by Dougie – and comedians such as Kenneth Williams and Frankie Howerd both admitted their debt to him.

Like many great performers Dougie was an outsider, in his case, a comedian on the edge of society. He lived alone and often performed on stage alone. He was his own invention. Sir John Betjeman, one of his champions, described him as 'a too little regarded genius'. Noel Coward admired him, so did Anthony Powell and Kingsley Amis. George Melly was a fan, so was Barbara Cartland. Even the late cookery writer Jennifer Patterson

Bawdy but British!

was prone to singing snatches of Byng material on TV's *Two Fat Ladies*.

Today Dougie Byng is virtually forgotten, all the more shameful since he was one of the biggest entertainment stars of his day. But, like certain others of his theatrical generation, he was not either a prolific film or TV star and preferred the lure of the stage.

In theory his legacy is a small one: a slim, sanitised but entertaining volume of autobiography – his sexuality was never mentioned throughout –, a collection of 78rpm recordings now happily transferred to CD, and the Feydeau farce film *Hotel Paradiso*, in which he played Monsieur Martin.

I knew Dougie for 17 years, both as a close friend and as his manager for his last performing years. He was a remarkable man – funny, witty, very kind and often outrageously difficult. And, like many great stage stars, he was larger than life – both on stage and off.

The quotes from Dougie in this book are taken from notes and diaries I kept during the time I knew Dougie and from his many letters to me – which are now housed in the British Theatre Museum. I have occasionally quoted from his autobiography and from one or two related magazine articles.

Patrick Newley

Following in Dougie's footsteps ~ Danny La Rue. Dougie once commented: 'I admire Danny because he, more than anyone, has brought glamour back to the theatre'.

Bawdy but British!

PART ONE

1.THE CATCH OF THE SEASON

Dressing up or wearing a costume was a vocation for Dougie Byng. In his long stage career he designed and wore an astonishing array of outfits ranging from spectacular pantomime dame finale dresses to comical home counties butler's outfits.

In revue he dressed up variously as Queen Boadicea, Doris, an ethereal goddess of wind, a Playboy bunny, a Norman castle, a burnt-out tree trunk, an Egyptian mummy and even Whistler's mother. On the cabaret floor in London's smartest nightclubs he sometimes appeared as an exotic orchid or as a bedraggled, ageing mermaid.

Off-stage no British stage star ever dressed more immaculately – or was more outrageously groomed. He rarely, if ever, wore casual clothes – it is impossible to imagine him in jeans and T-shirt – and was nearly always seen in green, red or mauve velvet suits. His ties were colourful, his cravats eye-catching. In 1961 Sir Alec Guinness noted in his diary: 'Spotted Dougie Byng on Brighton seafront wearing Russian hat with flowing mauve, silk scarf. Now that is eccentric.'

It is not surprising then that Dougie's earliest childhood memories were of sketching clothes and performing pantomimes on the top landing of the family home. 'I was always dressing up and being someone else,' he recalled. 'My first cabaret appearance was apparently in the drawing-room at about two years of age, standing on a hassock (stage sense now developing) reciting 'The Story of Mr Punch'. I vividly recall giving a rendering (still on a hassock) of *Twinkle, Twinkle, Little Star* – as it would be recited by a lady.'

His career as a songwriter also had its roots in childhood:

'At home, I was, on one occasion, whisked out from an evening party, for which, as a great treat, I had been allowed to stay up. I got the giggles as a large lady in white satin wearing pince-nez who, music in hand, gave us *'Every morn I bring thee violets'* with great gusto. She had very prominent teeth and as I was still a small boy (sitting on a chair) I had a worm's eye view of the dentures at every prolonged ah!-ah!-ah! I just couldn't stop laughing and was very quickly removed from the room by my embarrassed mother.

'This episode was the model for one of the first songs I wrote, *Spring* (Come out, come out, don't flop about, Spring is in the air.) and for that chestnut wig, pince-nez and the 'bust' which became my trademark in cabaret.'

The family home was in Nottingham where Dougie was born on 17 March 1893. His father was the managing director of the Midland Counties District Bank and his mother a former schoolteacher. It was a large and very Victorian family. When Dougie told his mother he wanted to be an actor, she replied stiffly, 'I hope, dear, you will never come to that.'

Dougie aged 2

Bawdy but British!

Dougie in character for his song 'Spring'

He attended Waverley Prep School, Stanley House and Clifton-ville but was hopeless at academic work and sports. His only real interest was showbusiness. His one theatrical effort at school, however, was not a success. At an end-of-term concert he played a commercial traveller trying to sell 'The Disinfected Doormat'. To add a touch of reality he arranged for friends scattered through the audience to open vials of ammonia at the critical moment. The rest of the audience fled in tears.

A teenage Nottingham friend of Dougie's was the future dame comedian Clarkson Rose. 'Douglas and I were about the same age,' he recalled. 'One day, when I had been invited round to the Byng's house for tea, Douglas and I, his brother Noel, and my cousins Muriel, Phyllis and Kathleen, formed ourselves into a concert party which we called The Eccentrics.

In concert party at Hastings 1914 aged 21

'Douglas and I quarrelled a little as to which of us should do the female impersonations. But his flair for this sort of thing was ahead of mine, he had all the props ready, and duly sang *I am the Catch of the Season*.'

When he was 16 Dougie went to Plouen in Saxony, where his older brother, Noel, owned a lace factory. There he studied music and the German language. On his return to England he made his first foray into show business when he went to work for the famous costume designer Charles Alias in Soho Square.

In 1914 he answered an advertisement in *The Stage* newspaper for a 'light comedian for a concert party by the sea – 28 week resident season' and was engaged by Greville Hayes, who managed the Periodicals Concert Party. Dressed in a farmer's smock with a red spotted handkerchief and singing *She's Fat and She's Beautiful* in a thick Somerset accent, he made his first appearance on stage at the Palacette, Hastings on 7 July 1914. The local paper said: 'Mr Byng proved a good comedian'.

'We did three shows a day,' said Dougie, 'and on bank holidays and special occasions, a show at eleven, one, three, five, seven and nine o'clock, changing the programme every three days. After that 'jump off', a year's tour with *The Girl in the Taxi*, a revival of the famous musical comedy. I played Professor Charcot, a French diplomat of 45 and later Herbert, the baron's son, aged 19.

'We played one, two, three night stands in town halls all over the country, often making up on the local Magistrate's bench, or even in the gents. Then the Gaiety Theatre in London (a big thrill). Thick carpets in the dressing rooms, and white seats backstage for the artists to rest on during 'waits' – clean evening-dress shirts, waistcoats, ties, collars, socks and handkerchiefs put out for you by your dresser for every performance, or thrice nightly if you wished it.'

Dougie did not fight in the First World War, because (a) he suffered from St Vitus' Dance, and (b) he described himself as being 'rather thin and weedy.' He may have been thin but early publicity shots of him show a handsome, self-assured, debonair figure. In later life he admitted to friends that he had known he was gay from a very early age and had been free from any sexual guilt, a remarkable attitude given the moral climate of Edwardian England.

Homosexuality then was regarded with abhorrence and the spectre of Oscar Wilde still lingered on long after his death in 1900. As a teenager, the flamboyant Anglo-Irish actor Micheal MacLiammoir, a friend and contemporary of Dougie's, innocently asked his father what Wilde's crime had actually been ? 'He was a moral leper,' fumed the father. 'And he was guilty of a far greater sin of going with bad women. He turned young men into women.'

Many people saw World War One as an opportunity to restore 'manly' Britain, to free it from decadent (ie. homosexual) influences. Lord Alfred Douglas, Wilde's former lover, now married and reborn as the great scourge of homosexuality, warned: 'It is just as important to civilisation that literary England should be cleansed of sex mongers and peddlers of the perverse, as that Flanders should be cleared of Germans.'

Dougie spent most of his early years on the road, touring provincial theatres, where he mixed with, and knew, other gay actors. There was a certain immunity from the outside world's moral backlash although as veteran director Frith Banbury commented: 'For quite a long time after the Oscar Wilde case, the leaders of the theatrical profession in London were fairly homophobic.'

In 1918 Dougie met Noel Coward for the first time. The two became life-long friends – and occasional lovers. 'I first met Noel when he was aged 19,' said Dougie. 'I was standing outside the stage door of the Shaftesbury Theatre in London and as he came towards me he suddenly did a sort of *entrechat trois* leap into the air with all the gay exuberance of youth he always had. I always felt that I would never be able to compete with all that vitality he had.'

Touring in 1920 Dougie played the juvenile lead, Christopher Deare, in *The Kiss Call* and at the Winter Garden, London the following year he was an understudy in *A Night Out*. At the age of 28 in 1921 he starred at the London Palladium as the Grand Vizier in *Aladdin*. He was back again on the road in several touring revues playing numerous characters. He adored the fun of touring but had little idea that within a year or two he would become one of London's biggest – and highest paid – names in entertainment.

2. THE MOST REFINED VULGARITY IN LONDON

As an entertainer in London during the late 1920s and throughout the 30s Dougie reigned supreme. This was his era and the one he would look back on, decades later, not only with affection but with great clarity. In the 1970s, when he was in demand as a raconteur on television, he would recall with ease the glittering West End nightclubs, society parties and luminaries such as Noel Coward, Cecil Beaton, Lady Diana Cooper, Tallulah Bankhead and many more.

'It was a mad, carefree world,' he said. 'No one imagined that there would ever be another world war. We were known as 'the Bright Young People.'

The Bright Young People were born out of the grief and social upheaval that followed the end of the First World War and their antics kept the press entranced at the time. Titled socialities began the vogue for practical jokes, treasure hunts and fancy dress parties. Stealing policeman's helmets and dancing all night at the Ritz was considered the norm. These were the first celebrities that were famous for being famous. George Orwell thought they had 'feathers for brains' but the Bright Young People had Evelyn Waugh and Nancy Mitford to fictionalise them.

Noel Coward ~ former lover of Dougie's. He described Dougie's cabaret act as 'the most refined vulgarity in London'

Bawdy but British!

Dougie, always an outsider, was not actually one of the Bright Young People himself but was adopted by them and was in demand to entertain them at parties. In later years, he was the inspiration for the effete cabaret artiste Max Pilgrim in Anthony Powell's saga *A Dance to the Music of Time*.

Dougie's big London break came in 1925 when he was taken on by the powerful producer C B Cochran. Cochran was an English Diaghilev, an impresario with a gift for spotting new talent and for bringing established names together in exciting combinations. He virtually invented revue before the First World War, moved on to cabaret in the twenties and formed a vital partnership with Noel Coward for a series of glittering shows including *Bitter Sweet*, *Cavalcade* and *Private Lives*.

He had seen Dougie's work in the provinces, admired his versatility, and decided to give him the role of lead comic in the new Coward revue, *On With The Dance*, which opened at the London Pavilion on 25 April 1925.

One of the sketches that Coward wrote for Dougie was called *Oranges and Lemons* in which Dougie and the eccentric, cavernous-faced Ernest Thesiger appeared as elderly spinsters preparing for bed in a Bloomsbury boarding house. Dougie played Grace who is 'rather set for maturity' and dressed in slightly matronly clothes. Thesiger, was Violet, the same age but skittishly dressed in a fringed tea-gown. Their sparring develops into bitchiness with Violet presenting herself as a woman of the world, Grace responding with middle class censoriousness:

Violet: *I must say this nightie was a bargain for £2/11d. I always like Liberty's.*
Grace: *I never allow them!*
Violet: *You probably did when you were my age.*
Grace: (looking under her bed before getting into it). *I always do this in case of cat burglars.*
Violet: *How droll of you. I'm never nervous of that sort of thing.*
Grace: *Indeed!*
Violet: *I expect it comes of being so cosmopolitan.*

Midnight visitors hold no terrors for me.
Grace: I should be more inclined to conceal that fact
than boast of it. Good night!

Later, two men stumble into the darkened room and try to get into bed and it is Violet who panics and Grace who offers the welcome.

On With The Dance was a huge success. The French star Alice Delysia sang *Poor Little Rich Girl* to Hermione Baddeley and there were two ballet sequences from Leonide Massine. Also in the cast were impressionist Florence Desmond and future Hollywood star Nigel Bruce. On the opening night finale there were endless curtain calls. The revue ran for 229 performances at the Pavilion, where the *Morning Post* acclaimed this 'decadent and brilliant show.'

Dougie remained with Cochran for five years, playing in *Still Dancing*, Cochran's 1926 Revue, *One Damn Thing After Another*, *This Year of Grace*, *Wake Up and Dream* and Cochran's *1930 Revue*. He played over 100 parts and regarded the London Pavilion as a kind of university. 'We were a sort of large family of children and Cockie, as some of us were privileged to call him, the biggest child of all,' he said. 'Every show he put on became a great new adventure because of his tremendous enthusiasm, our excitement about what we would get to do and the thrill of hearing at the band call the music by Noel Coward, Cole Porter or Rogers and Hart, or seeing the lovely sets and costumes by Cockie's newest finds, Oliver Messel or Gladys Calthrop. Once you had seen a Cochran revue all others seemed tawdry by comparison.'

During those five years, Dougie had amassed enough money to open his own nightclub off St Martin's Lane called the Kinde Dragon. He decorated it as a hostelry with settles, antique chairs and cutlery that included bone handled knives and forks. Although it attracted a gay element it was not a gay club, and it was here, along with friends such as Naunton Wayne, Florence Desmond and Gertrude Lawrence, that he would entertain late at night after appearing in the Cochran revues. It was also the place

In 1920s London the boundaries between straight and gay men as well as masculinity and sexuality were completely different than today. Although there were men who were only interested in having sex or romance with men, there were others who were happy to do so some of the time. Then, when they decided to get married, they did so and moved on. Sometimes they remained close friends with their male ex-partners. Dougie never described himself as 'gay'. He variously claimed he was 'a male mistress' or that he had had 'a number of affairs with male mistresses' during his lifetime.

Perhaps one of his most unlikely lovers was the hard-drinking actor Robert Newton, best known nowadays for his barnstorming role as Long John Silver in the 1954 film of *Treasure Island*. Dougie had met Robert in the early twenties before the actor had found film fame and was playing small roles in the West End.

'Bobby was a fascinating and delightful character who was not only 'with it' as regards casual clothes, he was ahead of it,' said Dougie. 'He was the first young man I saw in a light fawn corduroy suit with a pink shirt and bright green tie with a sort of Tyrolean hat showing his jet black curly hair. He looked like a mischievous boy from an Italian oil painting.'

Newton was known for throwing wild parties at his London flat. 'Bobby would collect all sorts of strange people on his way home if he felt like giving a party,' said Dougie. 'If they were lying in the gutter, he thought they needed cheering up.'

Newton went on to marry four times and died of alcoholism in 1956, aged 51.

Although Dougie's cabaret performances were frequented by rich socialites and dowager duchesses (his autobiography is knee-deep in long forgotten titles and social lions) the nature of his material attracted gay men. The bisexual writer and musician George Melly once told me that, 'going to see Dougie Byng in cabaret was a good place to meet other gay men. You would always end up in bed with someone.' In the sixties the same thing would happen at Judy Garland concerts.

Terrence Rattigan in 1930. Douglie embarked on an affair with him the previous year.

Terry

1930

In 1929 Dougie met and embarked on an affair with the future playwright Terence Rattigan, then aged 19. At 16, Rattigan, a tall and strikingly handsome youth, created a scandal at Harrow when he had a threesome with a local bookmaker and the racing correspondent of the *Daily Express*. His academic ability and promise at cricket saved him from expulsion.

Eyebrows were raised even higher when Rattigan took a group of Harrovians to the Cafe de Paris where Dougie was appearing in cabaret. Jimmy Stow, a former pupil at Harrow, said: 'Terry rather liked all that, the groups of homosexual men. He always used to say that the Greeks had a good attitude towards sex, which the British people didn't apparently have.'

Frank Rattigan, who bitterly opposed his son's intention to become a writer and insisted that he should follow him into the Diplomatic Service, was shocked by the meeting with Byng.

He was outraged still further when Terry, at Trinity College, Oxford, with a history scholarship, gave drag performances of his own as a bitchy female character he had invented, Lady Diana Coutigan (the surname was based on the expression 'queer as a coot').

Dougie standing on the famous staircase at London's Cafe de Paris in 1952. He was the Cafe's most consistent attraction over a period of 30 years

The nightclub that Dougie was synonymous with throughout his career was the Cafe de Paris in Coventry Street off Leicester Square. The club was opened by Poulsen, the Danish head waiter from the Embassy Club, and quickly became the fashionable and very expensive rendezvous for the new elite. The underground, oval-shaped room was a macabre choice in decoration, being a replica of the palm court of the ill-fated Luisitania, with a balcony round it and a double staircase curving down to the dance floor. This, however, formed a stylish background for cabaret artists such as Bea Lillie and Sophie Tucker, but it was Dougie who was the Cafe's biggest draw returning time and time again.

Billed by the Cafe management as 'London's Most Important and Expensive Cabaret Star' he was paid a staggering £300 per week in 1930, often appearing for six weeks at a time. In 1930 the average weekly earnings for a British man were 56 shillings or 17 shillings a week for unemployment benefit.

Night after night the Cafe was overflowing with the rich and famous but the most distinguished visitor was HRH Prince George, Duke of Kent. Prince George always attended when Dougie was appearing and often requested songs he liked best from Dougie's repertoire.

'He stopped me in Bond Street one morning,' said Dougie. 'He said, 'You've never written a yachting song'. I said, 'Well, I will if I can put your photograph on the cover if it is ever published.' I had a letter in my wallet and he wrote on the back of it, placed on my bowler hat, which I held, some lines from a song he knew when he was a naval cadet at Osborne.'

A wet sheet and a wind that's blowing fast.
And bend the jolly mast me boys and bend the jolly
mast.

Dougie's song began:

Hurrah for a blow on the ocean
And fun on the rolling sea.
You needn't fret if your sheets are wet,
As long as your wind blows free.

The Duke of Kent and Dougie were lovers. In his later years Dougie told me – and other friends – that he had 'dallied' with HRH. Indeed, even in old age, one of his most valued treasures was a silver-framed signed photograph of Prince George.

Fifth in line to succession to the throne, Prince George was created Duke of Kent in October 1934, in anticipation of his forthcoming marriage to Princess Marina of Greece and Denmark. The couple married in November 1934 in Westminster Abbey.

Described by one observer as 'cultivated, effeminate, and smelling too strongly of perfume' the Duke of Kent was the most intelligent member of his generation of the Royal Family. Before and after his marriage he had a string of affairs with both men and women, among the better known being Jessie Matthews, socialite Margaret Whigham (later the Duchess of Argyll), the black American singer Florence Mills and Noel Coward.

Coward's relationship with Kent, which lasted 19 years, was regarded as increasingly high risk during the Second World War and caused Coward to be placed under surveillance by the security services. They reported that Coward and Kent had been seen parading together through the streets of London, dressed and made up as women, and had once been arrested by the police for suspected prostitution.

Newspaper magnate Lord Beaverbrook, a member of Churchill's wartime cabinet, nursed a particular aversion to Coward and organised a theft from Coward's Belgravia home, 17 Gerald Road, of the Duke of Kent's passionate letters to Coward, one of which began, 'My dear, darling Noel' and another 'Noelie, my own sweet love'. The letters were kept in Beaverbrook's safe after the war but were nowhere to be found when Beaverbrook died in 1964.

The Duke of Kent was killed in a mysterious air crash in Scotland on August 23, 1942. Dougie was devastated when he heard the news. Official records of what happened appear to have vanished.

An equally distinguished admirer of Dougie's was Lady Elizabeth Bowes-Lyon, the future Queen Mother – who was a regular visitor to the Cafe de Paris and, in her later years, corresponded frequently with Dougie.

Elizabeth had always attracted the company of gay men. For a time, she was even a sort of gay sex symbol. In the late twenties and early thirties, at an annual London drag event known as Lady Malcolm's Ball, the Duchess of York was the subject of an uncannily accurate impersonation by one of London's leading transvestites. After Elizabeth's elevation to the throne, the same man continued his impersonation annually with increased regal overtones. From a chauffeur-driven Daimler would step a tiara'd and crinolined figure who appeared instantly recognisable. As passers-by burst into loyal applause, the guest-of-honour would adjust a white mink stole, gesture in a familiar style with a delicately gloved hand, incline a gracious head and then sweep up the steps.

'When Elizabeth was informed of this bizarre tribute, she was very amused,' said Royal biographer Michael Thornton. 'Homosexual humour was very familiar to her. A large number of the male friends she drew around her over the years – Harold Nicholson, Noel Coward, Benjamin Britten, Terence Rattigan – were homosexual. She had a civilised understanding of men whose relationships with women were only platonic. Many of her courtiers were lifelong bachelors. She used to refer to them as 'my knitting brigade'.'

Dougie appearing in cabaret in the 1930s.

In 1931 Dougie was invited to New York to appear in cabaret at a thousand dollars a week at the Club Lido. The advance publicity billed him as 'The highest paid English cabaret artist ever to go to the USA'. He sailed to New York on the Queen Mary with his regular accompanist Edward Cooper.

American audiences were impressed with his act and on opening night scores of celebrities turned out to watch him perform including New York Mayor Jimmy Walker, Fred and Adele Astaire, Dorothy Parker and Robert Benchley. One paper reported that his first appearance was 'without doubt one of the most beautiful openings we have attended with the glamorous background of this newly decorated room.' *The New York Evening Journal* called him a 'well set up Englishman, very glamorous' and yet another, 'a gifted fellow, an excellent comedian more diverting than many a nightclub entertainer I can think of.'

Dougie loved New York too – particularly Jazz Age Harlem which offered a combination of license and sexual ambiguity that provided a comfortable environment for gay men and women. Male impersonator Gladys Bentley performed at Harry Hansberry's Clem House; drag balls took place at the Rockland Palace and Savoy ballrooms. In the 'anything goes' atmosphere of Prohibition, private parties sprung up, part of an underground system that was ignored by the authorities. There were 'rent parties' known for their sexually charged atmosphere and bootleg liquor as well as 'buffet flats', apartments converted into sex clubs.

Ruby Waller, niece of blues singer Bessie Smith – recalled one buffet flat where there were 'nothing but faggots and bulldaggers . . . everybody that's in the life . . . everything goes . . . They had shows in every room, two women goin' together, and a man and a man goin' together . . . and if you were interested they do the same thing to you.'

Dougie was intoxicated with the liberated atmosphere and, as a visiting pro, was made welcome everywhere from the back street speakeasies to the world famous Cotton Club where he made friends with black stars such as Bill Robinson and Cab Calloway.

'I went to a lot of speakeasies with Jim Moriarty,' said Dougie. 'He ran the swish Chouette Club on East 61st Street. Jim would say, 'Don't anyone touch that!' when the drinks were bought, then he would strike a match and a blue flame would shoot out that almost reached the ceiling. Some people were just crazy and said, 'Oh hell, who cares?' and after drinking the raw alcohol went totally blind.'

Whilst in Harlem Dougie developed a sexual penchant for black men – which he maintained for the rest of his life.

Although he had enjoyed a string of discreet affairs in London Dougie was overwhelmed with the extraordinary sexual freedom that Harlem had offered him and, understandably, was extremely reluctant to return to London when his cabaret engagement was over.

'Time didn't exist in that smokey blue haze,' he said. 'Those nights in uptown Harlem were some of the most exciting and enjoyable moments that I have ever had. It was a new world for me and such a contrast to mixing with the Manhattan crowd. I was really living a double life and they might not have approved if they had known.'

Back in London he continued to appear in cabaret and was the first such artist to be hailed in neon lights in London, when his name shone in the gigantic advertisement for The Monseigneur on Piccadilly Circus.

By now he was one of Britain's wealthiest entertainers. He had a secretary, a chauffeur and car, and, when appearing in late-night cabaret in London, always stayed in a suite at the Hyde Park Hotel on Park Lane. In 1931 he had bought himself a large house named Wastlands in Mayes Green, Surrey. The house had several bedrooms, spacious grounds and a duck pond. Dougie was often photographed 'at home' for magazines such as *Tatler* and *The Sketch*.

In May 1932 he appeared at the Strand Theatre in *Duggy in Party* while continuing his late night cabaret, and in April 1933 he was at the Comedy Theatre in the impresario Andre Charlot's revue *How D' You Do*, with Frances Day and Edward Chapman.

Douglas Byng (right) as Boadicea with Frances Day as Poppaea and Edward Chapman as Nero in the sketch, 'Exposures', for which Byng wrote the lyric and music of "Boadicea's Song' in André Charlot's West End revue *How D'You Do?* which opened at the Comedy Theatre London on April 25 1933

Edward Chapman became a household name in the 1950s and 60s when he played Mr Grimsdale, the officious superior and comic foil to Norman Wisdom in Wisdom's popular film comedies but he also had a more dubious claim to fame. After Sir John Gielgud was arrested in October 1953 for 'importuning male persons for an immoral purpose' Chapman started a petition to force him to resign from Equity, the actors trade union. Sir Laurence Olivier reportedly threw Chapman out of his dressing room when he solicited his signature for the petition.

Chapman, somewhat surprisingly, eventually retired in the 1960s to live in Brighton, then as now, a city popular with gays and theatricals. Renowned for his rude behaviour he was dubbed by local taxi drivers as 'the pig of Brighton'.

Dougie preferred Charlot's revues to C B Cochran's. Charlot had introduced the intimate revue to London during the first world war but his were less structured. 'I was never given full scope at the London Pavilion with Cochran' said Dougie, 'although I played over one hundred character parts, male, female and neuter. Charlot gave me a lot of freedom and I was able to sing my own songs.'

Dougie's revue gallery of baroque females and grotesques included Flora MacDonald, Naughty Nellie Gwynn, Nana of the Manor, and many more. These characters were memorable not least because Dougie wore full drag, something he never did in cabaret. His revue costumes were outrageous, glamour crossed with the traditional pantomime dame, and this visual impact, together with his neurological twitch, gave the characters a crazy distinction. Hermione Gingold on speed, perhaps.

In *Hi-Diddle-Diddle* he introduced to British audiences for the first time Cole Porter's *Miss Otis Regrets*, a butler's apology for the absent murderess and, in the same revue, he also sang in praise of the charms of a cheap runabout 'flivver' who had seen better days – Henry Ford's Tin Lizzie Model T motor car, or some model of similar age and beauty.

Later, in *How D' You Do*, there was another non-drag number, *I'm A Tree,* in which he appeared as an ancient, gnarled, leafless tree trunk. It became one of his most celebrated numbers, even though it was bizarrely banned by the BBC in the 1930s after some listeners objected to the word 'gawd' in the lyrics. Recognition of the song came from an expedition descending Mount Everest. No one had seen anything but white snow and ice for weeks, but when one of the climbers saw a barren old tree trunk silhouetted against the sky he shouted, 'Oh look, there's Dougie Byng!'

I'M A TREE (Extract)

1.

To think that I should ever be,
Just nothing better than a tree;
Stuck here in lonely solitude,
So old and shivering in the nude,
Without a leaf to form a verdant cloak,
It's not a joke to be a blasted oak.

Refrain:

I'm the tree that the virgin queen once hid in,
I'm the tree that the gypsy left a kid in.
I'm a tree, never mind how chill the air is,
Nudists dance around me shouting,
'We believe in fairies'.
Just a tree, I was once a tree of knowledge,
A tree by which young men climbed in at college.
A tree that tramps encamp against, their shabby
    clothes unpinning,
A tree that lovers lean against when spring is just
    beginning,
You really must admit I'm more sinned against than
    sinning.
Gawd knows why I'm a tree.
A tree that every pussy cat each morning comes and
    claws at,
A tree that every water rat each evening comes and
    gnaws at;
A tree that for some reason every dog decides to pause
    at.
Gawd knows why I'm a tree.

Dougie performing '*I'm a Tree*' on BBC's *Before the Fringe 1967*. He had first performed the song in 1933.

Week-end parties, fancy-dress parties, swimming pool parties and charity balls were a fixtures of London society in the twenties and thirties. Frederick Ashton was in demand for his witty impersonations of Sarah Bernhardt and Sir Thomas Beecham, the Sitwells recited poetry or made pungent comments on their friends and enemies. Cecil Beaton photographed everyone.

One of the most prominent personalities of the period was the self-styled 'Queen of romance', Barbara Cartland, then a society gossip columnist on the *Daily Express*. She published her first novel, *Jigsaw*, a society thriller, in 1923 and went on to write an astonishing 1000 more books, nearly all of them best selling bodice-rippers. She and Dougie became lifelong friends – she referred to him as 'the wittiest man in London' – and he was often a fixture at her lavish parties. Years later, in her eighties, she described these parties to me as being 'nothing short of licentious orgies, full of naked men and dope'.

The truth? Or wishful thinking?

She also wrote Dougie into many of her novels. Leading characters would dine at the Cafe de Paris or The Monseigneur and 'watch Dougie Byng in cabaret'.

Charity balls attracted some of the biggest names in entertainment and were often held at vast venues such as Londonderry House or Grosvenor House. The most famous charity ball was staged at Grosvenor House in July 1935 by C B Cochran in aid of the Actors Benevolent Fund. While on holiday in Morocco, the great showman had discovered a fifteen-year-old Berber girl from the Atlas mountains. Olive-skinned and dark-eyed, she was a stunning beauty. Cochran decided to introduce her at the Grosvenor House ball as 'the most beautiful girl in the world'. She would be unveiled by some of London's most famous actresses.

Unfortunately, after enormous advance publicity, Abdaga decided not to come to London after all, leaving Cochran desperate for a substitute.

On the night of the ball Grosvenor House was packed with over 2000 people including HRH the Prince of Wales. Cochran's show had already run for four hours when the moment arrived to unveil 'Abdaga'. Fanfares sounded and there appeared a golden palanquin designed by Oliver Messel bearing a mysterious veiled figure. Gertrude Lawrence removed a veil, so did Tilly Losch and Dorothy Dickson. Clare Luce removed another. When all the veils had been taken off, out skipped, in full drag, Dougie Byng who sang *I'm the Bod*, a parody of Cole Porter's then current hit *You're the Top*.

The audience, accepting the hoax, erupted with laughter and cheered Dougie. The papers the next day described the event as 'the best kept theatrical spoof in years.

WHAT C. B. COCHRAN FOUND IN THE ATLAS MOUNTAINS!

Dougie revealed as the spoof 'Abdaga ~ the most beautiful girl in the world', Grosvenor House 1935.

As a cabaret star and revue artiste Dougie might not have seemed a natural bill topper in variety but in the heydays of the genre he was one of the biggest draws, in company with stars such as Nellie Wallace, George Robey and Gracie Fields. During the 1930s he commanded £125-£150 a week on the Moss Empire circuit.

He made his first appearance in variety at the Alhambra Theatre, Leicester Square, in a pantomime burlesque which he had originally written for Ivor Novello's birthday party. The skit became hugely popular and was his most requested spot in variety. It included the audience participation number, *Who'll Come and Roll Mother's Pudding?* – ' . . . *Daddy is out in Australia*; Granny has papered the tin; so if you're all good, you shall all have some pud: now who'll stick the first currant in?'

'I did my one man pantomime in practically every music hall in the British Isles,' he said. 'Any success I had was largely due to my agent Audrey Thacker who always managed to persuade Cissie Williams to book me. As it was always twice nightly, it was imperative that each performance run for a specified time, or the first house would be trying to get out as the second was trying to get in. You were allocated so many minutes for your act and no more. I once got a letter from Miss Williams telling me I was doing a minute less.'

Variety theatres often kept revealing reports of visiting acts. Most reports about Dougie's appearances were favourable towards his act although some commented on his material:

Holborn Empire, 20.04.1936: 'Very clever artiste with a nice personality. Doing impersonations of pantomime artistes which are very clever but hardly appeal to the cheaper part of the theatre.'

Finsbury Park Empire, 23.02.42: 'Very well received. A very finished performance and although Mr Byng can get away with more suggestiveness than many of his contemporaries, I did think him a little too near the mark on some occasions for a cosmopolitan audience.'

Nottingham Empire, 28.05.45: 'Well received. Douglas Byng, whose one man pantomime, a solo burlesque of pantomime principal characters is mostly worked with an apron, wig and headgear except for the final character, a gorgeous burlesque of a big busted principal boy which raises some good laughter, all of which are accompanied by a story, song and dances. Clever, good light entertainment.'

But perhaps the most unexpected report comes from the Glasgow Empire, 27.08.45, a theatre which was widely regarded as 'the comic's graveyard'.:

'Excellent reception. Presenting his usual burlesque of pantomime characters which is well appreciated and gets big laughs'.

Dougie did several other acts in variety but perhaps the most spectacular was his rendition of *I'm Doris, The Goddess of Wind* in which he was flown on stage in full drag on a wire.

Manager's Report — Douglas Byng (handwritten)

HALL	DATE			SALARY
MANCHESTER	13.4.36	Has a great sense of burlesque. His humour may be rather quiet for variety audiences but makes a good feature.	Yes	£150 £100 / £125
HOLBORN E.	20.4.36	Very clever artiste with a nice personality. Doing impersonations of pantomime artistes which are very clever, but hardly appeal to the cheaper part of the theatre. He goes well	No	£125 £70
GLASGOW E.	18.5.36	Impersonations are very well done, and is also a novel form of female impersonator	Yes	£130 80% £60
BHAM H.	25.5.36	His particular type of humour makes a strong appeal to the better parts of the house with whom he appears very popular	Yes	£125 £100 £100
HOLBORN E.	15.6.36	Puts up a very well thought out act of principles, in pantomime that is full of humour	Yes	£125 £55
PALLA.	6.7.36	An excellent act put over very neatly	Yes	£125 £100
B'HAM Roy.	28.9.36	Gets the best receptions; he is a good hardworking comedian		
B'ham Rep.	5.10.36	Appearing in 2nd week " a magnum of Charlot"		
PALLA.	19.7.37	Doing his burlesque pantomime with his customary artistry		16.8. 150.

DORIS THE GODDESS OF WIND (extract)

I'm Doris the Goddess of Wind,
A wind both rough and rude
They say I'm even more unkind
Than man's ingratitude.
I'm really not an ill wind,
Though I don't get any thanks,
For being, well, a frolic wind,
Just one of nature's pranks.
I put things in a whirl,
I'm just a naughty little girl.

I'm Doris the Goddess of Wind.
I make all sorts of things come unpinned.
I rustle the newspapers all over town,
And just after breakfast attack Major Brown,
I'm Doris the Goddess of Wind.
And I don't care a puff when I've sinned.

I blow through the bedrooms and blow out the light,
I blow to the left and I blow to the right,
My life's just one blow through from morning till
    night,
It's the wind, it's the wind.

Like all variety pros of the twenties and thirties, Dougie encountered his fair share of grotty digs and offbeat landladies.

'Landladies always seemed obsessed with the death of dear ones, especially if they had lost their husbands,' he said. 'Oh Mr Byng, he made a lovely corpse, just like suet' or 'I do wish you'd seen my husband when he was dead. He's just been to Blackpool – he did look well. '

'One landlady told me she had been to a sort of spiritualist meeting where they all took on each other's ailments. 'Mrs Johnson took on my bad knee and I took on her sore throat, but she left before I could give it back to her and so I've had it for a fortnight'.

Bizarre landladies or not, Dougie was very much at home in variety and enjoyed the camaraderie between fellow pros backstage. He loved working with the eccentric comedienne Nellie Wallace. Reg 'Confidentially' Dixon was a close friend. So was Stanley Holloway. 'We were all out for the same thing,' he said, ' the success of the show.'

Once, when appearing at the London Palladium in variety with Lorna and Toots Pounds he spotted Marie Lloyd:

'Lorna and Toots and I were rushing through the back of the stalls after a matinee and we almost knocked over Marie Lloyd who had just watched the show. She was wearing a moleskin coat with an enormous grey fox collar and a hat bursting with birds of paradise. As we went by, Lorna said, 'Hello Marie, working?' and Marie, pointing to all her finery shouted after us, 'Working? How do you think I got all this?' '

Dougie's top billing in variety was largely due to his many appearances on radio and early television which, by now, had made him a household name. Television shows were then broadcast live from Alexandra Palace and in 1938 Dougie starred in his own one-off series, *Byng-Ho*. Although he has been credited as the first female impersonator to appear on television, like his cabaret appearances he did not appear in full drag.

Comedian Bob Monkhouse remembered seeing Dougie on early television 'singing something my mother said was much too rude for children to hear. For years afterwards, whenever my parents were whispering, I would ask, 'are you doing a Douglas Byng?'

Dougie's career in theatre saw him work in many areas of light entertainment but to the general public he was best known as a leading pantomime dame. 'When I die,' he told me wistfully in 1981, 'there will be a small paragraph in the papers which will read, 'panto dame dead'. He was wrong, of course, because he got large obituaries that listed all his achievements but many people still associate his name purely with pantomime.

Many panto fans argue that he was the greatest dame of them all. Others have said that he was too sophisticated for the genre and was nothing like a traditional dame. He himself regarded George Lacey as the greatest dame and the two were friends for many years.

Traditional or not, he appeared in 27 pantomimes, many of which he received top billing over the title. The pantomimes were often produced by Prince and Emile Littler or Howard & Wyndham and were lavish with leading support acts and a full orchestra. Some pantomimes even boasted a 20-girl dance troupe.

Dougie took the art of pantomime very seriously, as seriously as a straight actor would Shakespeare. '*Mother Goose,*' he said, 'is the *Hamlet* of pantomimes.' He also had strong views on how to actually 'play' pantomime: 'You don't play in profile, you play everything front on, straight out to the audience. You've got to maintain the illusion – I would never take my wig off at the end, for the walk-down; you must stay in character.'

In the history of pantomime he was the first performer to 'glamorize' the dame. The dame proper was a direct result of music hall in the late 19th century, the most famous of which was the brilliantly eccentric comic Dan Leno. Leno's impersonation of women was described by a contemporary critic as 'the lodging house and slavey type' and the majority of dames of this period and just after – George Robey and Wilkie Bard to name but two - reveal a similar direction: a plain skirt, an apron or shawl, sturdy boots and her hair parted severely in the middle.

The *grande dame* was invented by Dougie. 'I was always a snob about my dames,' he said. 'I refused to be the cook or a nursemaid, and insisted on being Alderman Fitzwarren's housekeeper, or a governess to the babes in the wood.'

A rare photo of two of Britain's greatest panto dames ~ the late Jack Tripp (L) and Welsh comic Wyn Calvin. Tripp had served his apprenticeship in panto playing 'son' several times to Dougie's Dame. *'Dougie was the greatest Dame of them all'*, said Tripp.

Whatever the subject he was able to dress and behave like a regal duchess or bejewelled dowager, often caricaturing his own smart set cabaret audiences. Of the dame role itself he said, 'You can be more saucy as a woman than as a man. 'What he did to me' is very different from 'what I did to her'. She's on the DEfensive. A man's on the OFFensive.

'One or two managements said I was too sophisticated for a children's show. I always did one joke for the children and one for the grown-ups and the grown-ups laughed at the one for children and vice-versa.'

As usual he designed his own costumes whether they were comic or glamorous.

'I was once given a hat by a friend of mine who had worn it at Ascot. It was the first hat to be made of perspex and I thought it would be useful in pantomime. I decorated it with a pineapple, apples, grapes and bananas and it looked like a round dish of fruit. I thought I was being very original, only to find a book on pantomime with a picture of the famous clown Joe Grimaldi wearing a suit made entirely of vegetables more than two hundred years ago.'

Dougie also designed a frying pan hat, complete with eggs and bacon and, mocking the 1930s fashion for short fox-fur capes made out of single skins, had a cape made entirely out of loofahs. When the Second World War broke out, these bathroom accessories soon became unobtainable and much sought after, so much so that he was forced to keep his cape locked up so that people couldn't steal the loofahs.

He had first appeared as a dame in pantomime in 1924 at the New Oxford Theatre in London playing Eliza. It was here that he performed his comic routine of dressing the kitchen with the clothes he was wearing – his skirt made the table-cloth, handbag a vase for the flowers on his hat, which made a tea cosy for the teapot. In fact, he was largely responsible for establishing the tradition that the dame should wear increasingly flamboyant and outrageous costumes, which now provides one of the characteristic running gags of modern panto.

Dougie seen in typical pantomime finale dress ~ which he designed himslef. The silver bow was bequethed to Danny La Rue in Dougie's will.

His finale dresses were legendary – black satin or silk flowing gowns worthy of Norman Hartnell, elaborate feather headdresses crowning a mass of blonde hair, 20ft trains made of ostrich feathers – audiences, particularly in the north, would gasp as he descended down a staircase to the footlights. 'I wanted every lady in the audience to want to go out and buy one of my finale dresses for themselves,' he said.

His penchant for glamour, however, was never at the expense of the comedy in a pantomime and he relished the classic gags and knockabout routines. Always a physically fit performer he dashed out onto the stage with ease and changed costumes up to twenty times in a show. He wrote many of the scripts himself and, even in his seventies, often compiled dame gags in a series of notebooks for pleasure. These notebooks are now in the Theatre Museum Archive.

'The same pantomime gags have been getting laughs for years,' he said. 'But nobody knows who first cracked them. When the dame suddenly sees the demon king and shouts, 'Oh it's me late husband and I've spent the insurance money; and when the king and queen in the sleeping beauty scene wake up after a hundred years and the queen says, 'oh dear, I've just thought of something. I never put the cat out' – these are still funny today and get a laugh.'

Once when playing the role of the Queen in *The Sleeping Beauty* he was asked in the interval to make a charity appeal to the audience. Horrified, he retorted that, as far as the paying customers were concerned, especially the children, he was asleep for a hundred years, and would not destroy the illusion.

Throughout the thirties he was one of the biggest earners in pantomime and starred all over the country: Wilhemena Whackster in *Babes in the Wood* (Birmingham 1935), *Babes in the Wood* (Leeds 1936, Edinburgh 1938, Manchester 1939) and Widow Twankey in *Aladdin* (Golders Green 1940).

A 1938 review in the *Edinburgh Evening News* of *Babes in the Wood*, a lavish production which included an aerial ballet and 16 Tiller Girls, gives an idea of his pantomime skills:

'From the moment that Douglas Byng alighted from his bicycle on the village green it was evident that the Dame was going to be the enlivening influence on the whole proceedings. Discussing his wardrobe before the show opened, Mr Byng remarked that he found it difficult to design hats that would be funnier than some worn by fashionable ladies nowadays. The spontaneous outbursts of laughter that greeted his many appearances in the course of the evening testified that he had succeeded to a marked degree.

'His dresses were correspondingly grotesque or neat in design as occasional demanded, and altogether his Dame was a triumph of make-up. His hunting song was a superb caricature, and when he took part with the robbers in a game of hide and seek in the nursery he showed that he possessed a fine understanding of real pantomime. Not to be outdone by the butterflies, he, too, did a spot of flying while he sang *I'm a Bird*'.

'Pantomime,' said Dougie, 'has always been taken much more seriously in the provinces and you must play it seriously if it is to be a success. Binnie Hale once told me that a man with his family in the dress circle one night laughed so much at the comics that he had a fit and died. He was removed to the chocolate kiosk in the interval and his wife, bending over him, said, 'Will those lips never speak to me no more?' When answered, 'I'm afraid not,' she replied, 'Well, I'd better get back to see the rest of the panto-mime.' Which she did.

It was at the Palace Theatre in July 1938 that Dougie played his favourite role in a musical. that of Prince Zorpan in *Maritza*. He wrote all his own part as well as two numbers for himself to Emmerich Kalman's music. In the cabaret scene he appeared as a female violinist and sang, '*I'm the pest of Budapest that turned the Danube so blue.*'

The Pest from Budapest from the musical
Maritza.

'It was the only time I ever 'stopped the show',' he said. 'I had allowed for an encore and written an extra chorus, but after several calls I went to my dressing room and was changing when the stage manager came and made me take another call in my dressing gown, of which I didn't really approve, but secretly enjoyed. No wonder Herr Kalman said to me afterwards, 'It's not *Maritza* as I know it. but very funny.' '

By the end of the thirties the bright young people began to disperse. The depression, fascism and in increasing awareness that their generation was being drawn into a world war made some grow up. Reality could no longer be ignored.

Many, including showbiz performers, began to be aware of the suffering inflicted by the Nazis. In the summer of 1938 Dougie had joined an all-star cast at the Gaumont State Cinema, Kilburn in a charity show supporting Eddie Cantor's appeal of behalf of Jewish refugees from Germany and Austria. The performers were included Cantor himself, Gracie Fields, Vera Lynn, Max Miller, Flanagan and Allen, George Formby and Bea Lillie.

London night life continued to flourish and those who could afford it still wined and dined at the Cafe de Paris or the Monseigneur. On the night that World War Two was declared Dougie was playing in non-stop revue at the Prince of Wales Theatre. The show closed at eight when orders came through that all the lights were to be extinguished as an air raid on London was likely to happen.

Dougie quickly phoned his sister, Amy, and asked her to travel down with him to his cottage in Surrey. In the car Amy complained bitterly that she had forgotten to bring her favourite laxative, Alophen, with her. 'Listen, dear, 'said Dougie. 'If a bomb drops near us, you won't need Alophen.'

Clarke Hutton's illustration for *Naughty Victoria Days*
published in *More Byngs Ballads* (1935)

Clarke Hutton's illustration for *I'm a Tree*
published in More *Byngs Ballads* (1935)

Bawdy but British!

Clarke Hutton's illustration for *Millie the Mermaid*
published in *Byngs Ballads* (1933)

Clarke Hutton's illustration for *Nanna of the Manor*
published in More *Byngs Ballads* (1935)

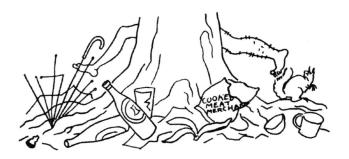

3. BAWDY BUT BRITISH!

Dougie was one of the busiest and most prominent entertainers during World War Two, dividing his time between West End revues, variety, cabaret and entertaining the troops for ENSA (christened 'Every night Something Awful' by Tommy Trinder) both at home and in the Far East.

ENSA (Entertainment National Services Association) was established just before the war to provide a variety of entertainment for the troops and other war workers serving both on the home front and overseas. It was managed by the theatre director Basil Dean from Drury Lane and operated on all war fronts.

At the beginning of the war Dougie told the management of the Cafe de Paris to change his current billing from 'The one and only Douglas Byng' to the more patriotic 'Douglas Byng – Bawdy but British!' and in cabaret he now wore an ordinary dinner jacket rather than full evening dress. He also wrote a new song, *Blackout Bella*, which he sang at every troop concert.

'Blackout Bella was about a wartime tart in the blackout' said Norman Hackforth, one of Dougie's regular accompanists. 'Dougie's costume was outlined in luminous paint, and for the last chorus he paraded in a blackout with a luminous banner which read: 'Hello dearie!'

On the opening night at the Cafe this stopped the show and continued to do so ever after.'

I'm Blackout Bella, the whitest girl in town.
A girl who knows the game,
Who's groped her way to fame,
Every fella salutes me on the beat,
Doing a bomps-a-daisy all down Regent Street.
I've popped in here, but not to profiteer,
My cover charge is less than half-a-crown.
I'm the only bag of lard that doesn't need a ration card,
I'm Blackout Bella, the whitest girl in town.

On one of Dougie's first ENSA tours he was sent to Scapa Flow in company with Tommy Trinder, Bea Lillie and Norman Hackforth. The company performed sketches and Dougie appeared as an ATS officer talking to an Army officer: 'It's no good your boys chasing our girls, Major. Oh, no. Our girls have got it here.' And he would tap his forehead with a finger. 'It doesn't matter where your girls have got it,' replied the Major, 'my boys will find it.'

Dougie's material proved popular with the troops but not everyone was happy. 'At one troop concert in Llanelli I went down so well I had to make a speech at the finish of my act,' he said. 'I had been there thirty years before in my first musical and I said how glad I was to be there again and hoped to come back another time. The voice of a sergeant was heard to say, 'He'll never come back here again, if I have anything to do with it.'

At another concert a Brigadier was overheard to say, 'If my daughter had been here, I'd have shot that Byng fellow.'

Sexual licence was very much to the fore during World War Two, especially in London during the Blitz. Quentin Crisp, recalled that 'For most of 1940 London by night was like one of those dimly-lit parties. As soon as the bombs started to fall, the city became like a paved double bed. Voices whispered suggestively at you as you walked along. Hands reached out to you if you stood still.'

Dougie told me that during this period he had enjoyed more anonymous sexual trysts than he had since his first visit to Harlem.

'People were in different circumstances,' explained theatre director Frith Banbury, a close friend of Dougie's. 'They were away from their families so the what-will-the-neighbours-say factor didn't come into it. And there were lots of foreigners – Poles, Czechs, the French – all round the place there was a good deal of sex to be had from people who were on the loose.'

Gay actor and ENSA artiste Phill Grainger was taken by his Royal Marines cousin to London clubs such as The Golden Garter and The Cafe Anglais – where Dougie was a regular attraction. 'Great fun it was in those days,' he said. 'It was more exciting because it was illegal, I suppose,'

Dougie was in London for most of the Blitz, appearing in pantomime at Golders Green Hippodrome as well as doing troop concerts with the likes of Fred Emney and Richard 'Mr Pastry' Hearne.

He was also doing short seasons at the Cafe de Paris, the Cafe having reopened during the Blitz because it was situated underground beneath the Rialto cinema and was considered London's safest restaurant.

Disaster struck, however, on the night of 8 March 1941. The place was packed with fashionable society and officers on leave, all bent on forgetting the horrors of war. At around a quarter to ten, Snakehips Johnson and his band were launching into *Oh Johnny* when two bombs plunged through the Rialto roof and straight into the Cafe killing 34 people, including Snakehips, and another member of the band. 60 were seriously wounded.

Dougie had been appearing at the Cafe for three weeks and had several more to go. On the night of March 8th he was appearing earlier in the evening in revue at the London Coliseum. On leaving the Coliseum to make his way to the Cafe he was delayed by air raids and he and a friend sought shelter in a restaurant in St Martin's Lane. By the time they arrived at the Cafe the place had been devastated.

Rescue workers arrived amid scenes of macabre horror. One woman recalled having her leg bathed in champagne. Another, sprawled wounded and semi-conscious over the corpse of an officer, felt a looter slipping the rings off her fingers.

'The table at which I always had my supper was on the part of the balcony that crashed down onto the crowded dance floor where all the people were killed,' said Dougie. 'Many had their money and jewellery stolen, as they were dying, by the vultures in the demolition and rescue squads who also looted all the showcases in the entrance within minutes of the explosion.

'Of course everyone thought I was there and I was opening letters and telegrams and answering phone calls for days. And I had a nasty delayed reaction after it was all over with the thought of so many people who had perhaps come specially to hear me – which made it seem such a very personal tragedy.'

A wartime photo of Dougie singing 'Mont-martre'.

Nearly all light entertainment did well during the war but perhaps the most surprising thing was the great popularity with the troops of the more sophisticated intimate revues. *Fine and Dandy* (1942) saw Dougie in company with Leslie Henson and Stanley Holloway and a year later he topped the bill in *Flying Colours*. The latter, an H M Tennant revue, is particularly notable in that Dougie was to have sung Noel Coward's infamous wartime song, *Don't Let's Be Beastly To The Germans*. The number was printed in the programme but was cut at the dress rehearsal on the instructions of Coward because of a misguided public furore over its lyrics. Coward was later very careful, in his own spoken introductions, to make the point that it was a satirical song. Revue fans can only wonder what the Byng rendition might have sounded like.

> *Let's be sweet to them,*
> *And day by day repeat to them*
> *That sterilization simply isn't done.*
> *Let's help the dirty swine again*
> *To occupy the Rhine again*
> *But don't let's be beastly to the Hun.*

In 1944 Dougie was sent by ENSA on a gruelling tour of the Far East to entertain troops in India, Burma and Singapore. It was no mean feat for a man then aged 51. Kitted out with a mosquito net and toilet rolls, the latter not being obtainable in India, he sailed on a troopship convoy and after four weeks docked in Bombay.

Conditions for entertainers were just as rough as they were for the troops and it was hard work, travelling bumpy roads over long distances and sleeping in bamboo huts in the jungle areas.

The heat was unbearable. Vera Lynn recalled the slap of the huge jungle insects dive-bombing her accompanist's keys as they honed in on the lights of her improvised stage. 'It was a bit warm doing my one man pantomime wearing the Principal's Boy's bust over a dinner jacket with cotton tights underneath,' said Dougie. 'You sweated liked mad. But it was all very worthwhile.'

The troops in Burma and India had been starved of entertainment and ENSA shows were a rarity. It must have come as a shock, therefore, to some of them to be suddenly presented with Dougie's outrageous female-impersonation type of act in the middle of the jungle, miles from London's sophisticated West End.

The need in the Far East was for entertainers who could be mobile, go anywhere, do their stuff in a hospital ward, from a jeep, or on the top of a mountain pass. Actor Jack Hawkins, who took charge of ENSA in India and the Far East from 1944, said that in the outlying districts of India it was only the tireless work of artistes like Dougie and Joyce Grenfell, who were prepared to get on with the job they had been sent to do, that kept ENSA's reputation in good stead.

Dougie appeared in shows with Gracie Fields, Leslie Henson and the husband and wife double act Nan Kenway and Douglas Young, and, after Bombay, Bangalore, Hyderabad and Madras, found himself posted to Singapore where he was treated like a VIP and given a room at Government House.

'I slept in a huge bedroom with nothing it in but a small army bed covered with a mosquito net,' he said. 'The Japs had only just left and had stripped the place bare.'

He went on to reopen the famous Victoria Theatre in Singapore and then returned to Britain via Karachi and Cairo, giving more troop concerts along the way.

In Karachi he did a concert at a military hospital in company with the soprano singer Doris Ingram. 'I did one ward and she did another,' said Dougie. 'When she had finished she came to me and said, 'I can't think what happened. I was singing *Bless This House* and when I came to the line, 'Bless the people here within, keep them pure and free from sin', I got a huge laugh from all the boys.' I made some inquiries and found out she had been singing in the VD ward.'

When the war ended it was inevitable that he should go back to pantomime – this time top billed again as the Queen in *Sleeping Beauty* at the Birmingham Hippodrome.

Although the war was over there were still occasional troop concerts and in March 1947 Dougie agreed to do a Combined Serv-ices Entertainment concert party in

Stage and singing star Elisabeth Welch. She and Dougie survived a plane crash together.

Gibraltar with Elisabeth Welch, Kay Cavendish and Richard Hearne. But the party failed to arrive, having crash-landed near Cadiz: Elisabeth Welch recalled the incident:

'We took off from Croydon in a tiny airplane early one cold Sunday morning. Some hours later we were flying very low among some very sharp-looking Spanish mountains in a terrible storm. The radio was out of action, the rain was pouring in on us, our petrol was running low, and we were lost. At last we saw a bit of green below and the pilot decided we'd better try and make a landing. So we braced ourselves for a bang, but instead of that it was a dull plonk and we sank in mud up to the wing spread.

'Out we climbed onto the wing, green with fright, wet and very bedraggled. No wonder the locals stared. They'd struggled through the rain and mud up to our plane, but just stood staring. Not one of us knew a word of Spanish, so a series of miming, pidgin French and Spanish began. Finally we were taken through mud up to our knees to a little house where we were put around a table near a roaring fire. Joy of joys, there was also a charcoal burner under the table to warm our legs and a lots of children running about. They were very poor people, but offered us food which we refused, but we had some hot water and some wine to warm us.

'We somehow made them understand that we were artists, so of course they asked us to perform, which somehow we did. Then someone brought in a guitar and they proceeded to entertain us with all their wonderful flamenco singing and playing. They bedded us down late that night on the floor of that little house, but who could sleep after so much excitement?

'Richard Hearne and our pilot, Douglas Neill, waded three rivers to get to a phone. Exhausted, they sent an SOS to the British Consul at Cadiz. We were eventually rescued by a mule team, but we stayed with the villagers long enough to enjoy more flamenco singing. We rode two-to-a-mule to Algar whose 1500 strong population thronged to the main street to greet us. After drying out, we were treated to a huge banquet.'

4. BROADWAY TO BRIGHTON

By the late forties and early fifties Dougie was in danger of becoming almost theatrically 'respectable'. He starred in a series of West End musicals playing comic, but non-camp, roles that were a million miles away from his female grotesques. He did not, however, abandon either cabaret or revue completely where his 'ladies' flourished in songs or sketches.

I'M ONE OF THE QUEENS OF ENGLAND

This is my second time on earth,
At least it so appears.
I've mucked around in ether,
For about a thousand years.
I've been a ghost from time to time,
And others things as well,
But who, and when, and what I was,
I'm blowed if I can tell.

I'm one of the Queens of England,
But I can't remember which,
I know that Pa had Royal Blood,
And Ma was very rich.

I may be dear Queen Guinivere,
Who darned King Arthur's tights,
And cleaned up armour all the day,
For all those dirty knights

I may have been Queen Boadicea,
In ages past and gone.
I'll have a fight with anyone,
But not with nothing on.
I don't think I was Mary Tudor,
Mrs Phil of Spain –
I hope to Gawd I wasn't,
She had such a bloody reign.

I'm one of the Queens of England,
But I can't remember which,
Old Good Queen Anne ruled liked a man,
Things got to such a pitch,
I don't know who the hell I was
Or what I may have been,
But one thing's very certain,
I was not the Virgin Queen.

I'm one of the Queens of England,
But I can't remember which,
I wasn't Mary, William's wife,
Who won the Dunmow Flitch.
Henry the Eighth had several Queens,
Oh 'e was very 'ot,
So judging by what I can do,
I was all the blasted lot.

In May 1947 he starred as the Baron at the Palace Theatre in *The Bird Seller*, a musical which boasted an enormous orchestra conducted by Richard Tauber – but the show failed.

Dougie as Mrs Crusoe in *Robinson Crusoe* (Theatre Royal, Newcastle, 1954) with Lynette Rae (L) in the title role and principal girl Judith Whittaker (R)

GOLDERS GREEN
HIPPODROME

PROGRAMME
FOR WEEK COMMENCING MONDAY, NOVEMBER 22nd, 1948

6.15   VARIETY   **8.30**
TWICE NIGHTLY

1. OVERTURE	... ...	Van Dam and his Orchestra
2. RAVIC & RENEE	...	Whirlwind Acrobatic Skaters
3. THE THREE CALORES SISTERS		Earful of Music
4. CLIFFORD STANTON	...	Personalities on Parade
5. THE BOTONDS	... ...	Acrobatic Supermen

6. RICHARD MURDOCH		Of "Much-Binding-in-the-Marsh"
7. INTERVAL	... ...	Van Dam and his Orchestra
8. JACK CRISP & JILL	...	Everything in Dancing
9.	DOUGLAS BYNG	
	The Celebrated Revue and Cabaret Star	
	At the Piano: FREDDIE WHELDON	
10.	STEVE CONWAY	
	The B.B.C. Sweet Serenader and Columbia Recording Star	
	At the Piano: JACK MARKHAM	
11. REG DIXON	... ...	"Confidentially"
12. YALE & DIANE	... ...	Youth in the Balance

SMOKING PERMITTED IN THE AUDITORIUM.
FULLY LICENSED BARS IN ALL PARTS OF THE THEATRE.
NOTICE—PHOTOGRAPHING IN THIS THEATRE IS FORBIDDEN.
The Management reserve themselves the right to make any change, vary or omit any part of the Programme without previous notice.

Dougie on a variety bill 1954

Oklahoma! had opened two weeks previously and had changed the style of musicals.

Rex Jameson, later to find fame on stage as the gloriously boozy Mrs Shufflewick, had just been demobbed from the RAF when he saw Dougie in *The Bird Seller*. 'I remember being very struck by his performance,' he said. 'He had this tremendous vocal attack and stage presence. He was a big, big theatre star then, complete with all the trappings, a chauffeur to pick him up at the stage door and all that. Even when I met him for the first time, much later in the 1970s, I was slightly in awe of him.'

The following year Dougie returned to New York in cabaret and on his return was in demand again in variety.

One of the most famous fifties revues that he appeared in was *Sauce Piquante* in which he appeared with a cast of then up and coming stars – Moira Lister, Norman Wisdom and Bob Monkhouse. Joining them was a shy, young girl actress/dancer. Her name was Audrey Hepburn.

With her stunning elfin-like looks, Hepburn almost stole the show from the rest of the cast. One of her fellow dancers, a Scandinavian, Aud Johanssen, renowned for her magnificent bust, would come off-stage after every performance cursing: 'I can't stand it! I know I've got the best tits on stage, and yet they're all staring at a girl who hasn't got any.'

According to the then Prime Minister, Harold Macmillan, we'd 'never had it so good' in Britain during the fifties. But drab fifties Britain was not the place to be if you were homosexual. In the British establishment there was a deep vein of anti-gay prejudice. Homosexuality had not only been against the law, it had been actively prosecuted by the police. The defection to Moscow of British Foreign Office spies Burgess and Maclean was widely regarded as a conspiracy of left-wing 'queers'. The notorious reactionary

Home Secretary, Sir David Maxwell Fyffe, was convinced that homosexuality threatened the British way of life.

Egged on by the national press, he and his colleagues believed that they had a mission to liberate British society from these 'evil' men.

However, Michael Relph, who produced the groundbreaking film *Victim* (1961) – has pointed out that well known gay theatrical figures were relatively safe – providing they were discreet:

'In those days film directors such as Anthony Asquith and Brian Desmond Hurst, as well as Noel Coward and Ivor Novello, were protected by the theatrical world. There wasn't any harassment of gay people in our profession. However, a cat and mouse game existed with police if gays stepped outside their particular world. I remember when John Gielgud was caught cottaging in the early 1950s. Sometimes the police turned a blind eye because the law was transparently ridiculous and hypocritical as far as homosexuality was concerned. From their point of view, provided you didn't overstep the mark, they were quite tolerant. But the law that existed seemed distasteful and out of date to me.'

Dougie remained relatively discreet in his private life – although there were drawbacks. 'I was appearing in pantomime in the fifties in Harrogate,' he told me in 1977. 'One day I met a man I rather fancied and we arranged to meet after the evening show – in an alley – of all places – near the theatre. That night I was the last person to leave the stage door and I crept down a side turning to this alley for the rendezvous. As I stood there nervously in the dark I looked over at the theatre and saw my name top billed on all the posters. I thought, my god, if people could see me now lurking in this alleyway. But that's what it was like then. You had to be very careful.'

Career-wise, Dougie's longest running success – apart from his many seasons at the Cafe de Paris – was, ironically, not a drag role, but the part of Monsieur Martin, the excitable barrister who only stutters when it rains, in the Feydeau bedroom farce *Hotel Paradiso*. The play was presented by H M Tennant at the Winter Garden theatre (now the site of the New London Theatre) in May 1956 and boasted a spectacular cast including Alec Guinness, Irene Worth, Martita Hunt, Kenneth Williams plus the then relatively unknown Billie Whitelaw. Peter Glenville directed, Osbert Lancaster designed the clothes and Tony Armstrong-Jones (later Lord Snowdon) took the publicity photographs.

It was London's first taste of Feydeau and proved to be an instant smash. Dougie stole many of the notices, Caryl Brahms noting that he played

Martin 'with and elegance, style and panache that is one of the play's many distinctions.'

It was a classy production, a typical fifties product of HM Tennant. Billie Whitelaw recalled that director Peter Glenville always came to rehearsals immaculately dressed, 'as though he were off to Ascot in the afternoon.

Sir Alec Guinness at Dougie's memorial service at St Paul's Covent Garden. He and Dougie were close friends and appeared together in both stage and screen versions of the Feydeau farce *Hotel Paradiso*.

(photo: Colin Bourner)

I always felt that he should be rehearsing with a cigarette holder in his hand.'

When the play transferred to Broadway in 1957, Dougie was the only member of the London cast to go with it, Alec Guinness being replaced by Bert Lahr and Billie Whitelaw with a young Angela Lansbury.

A film was eventually made eight years after the original London opening, again with a stellar cast: Alec Guinness, Dougie, Gina Lollobrigida, Robert Morley, Akim Tamiroff, Robertson Hare, Peggy Mount, Derek Fowlds and Leonard Rossiter. Filmed in Paris during a heatwave, Eric Payne, one of Dougie's close friends visited the set. 'Dougie had this extraordinary energy for his age,' he said. 'The studio was sweltering and Dougie had this scene where he had to rush up and down a flight of stairs. Something kept going wrong technically and the scene had to be reshot several times. Dougie never complained at all, in fact he seemed to rather enjoy it.'

Many of the cast had happy memories of making the film. Dougie lunched regularly with Alec Guinness and struck up a friendship with the young Derek Fowlds. But the film itself proved to be a flop. The breathtaking speed and excitement of the original stage farce proved impossible to capture on film. Alec Guinness judged it as 'not good, a very flaccid and mistaken construction.' Nevertheless, it remains an invaluable and rare record of Dougie at work and it is not difficult to imagine the rounds of applause he would have received on his various comic entrances and exits in the original stage production.

There is a curious footnote to the stage version of *Hotel Paradiso*. Alec Guinness recalled that one night before the show Martita Hunt collared him in her dressing room and announced that one of the cast had 'no balls'. The actor was never mentioned by name but it appears that his testicles had never descended. 'Martita and I met again on stage and as Mr So-and-so made his entrance our eyes met and we both had barely controlled giggles', said Guinness. 'By the interval she was reconciled to the poor man's plight and whispered, 'Anyway, I think Mr So-and-so is a bugger, so it probably doesn't matter very much.'

Mr So-and-so was not Dougie – I saw him in the buff on many occasions backstage in the late seventies when he was doing his one man show – so who was the unfortunate ball-less actor? Kenneth Williams?

More West End stage shows followed for Dougie. In October 1959 he appeared in the ill-fated musical *The Love Doctor* with Ian Carmichael and Joan Heal. The show closed after 16 performances, having been judged old-fashioned and corny by the critics. The magazine *Plays and Players* explained: 'The Love Doctor was an unspectacular, unpretentious little musical comedy which would have given pleasure to thousands had it not been killed by the hypersensitive critics.' This time it was *West Side Story* which had altered critical taste.

At the Phoenix in October 1963 Dougie played General Kuitizky in *House of Cards* and toured the following year with John Hanson in *The Maid of the Mountains*. He took over from Wilfrid Hyde-White in a star studded production of *Lady Windemere's Fan* – the cast included Isobel Jeans and Coral Browne with sets by Cecil Beaton – at the Phoenix in 1967 and toured the next year as Sir Jasper Fidget in *The Country Wife* with Julia Foster.

As ever, his songs remained a key part of his career and in 1967 he sang several of his compositions on the BBC2 series *Before the Fringe* and two year later recorded, with a full orchestra under the direction of Eric Rogers, an LP, *Douglas Byng Looks Back*.

FAMILY HEIRLOOM

1.

On with the motley, on with the dance,
Let joy be unconfined.
For life is just a game of chance,
With memories entwined.
The past is mirrored in a haze,
Yet sometimes there appears
A little like with bygone days,
To charm the passing years.
From a tall-boy in the spare room,
Where each night it goes to rest,
Comes a small but treasured heirloom,
And the one I love the best.

Refrain:
It's the only bit of ermine in the family,
A relic of those noble days of yore.
It first started as a spread
On King Charles the Second's bed,
Though by morning it was mostly on the floor;
Then on one of Nell Gwynne's gowns,
Well, it saw its ups and downs;
Till the merry monarch caught it in a door.
It was worn beneath the belt,
And poor Nellie lost her pelt;
Still it's clothes that make the lady, nothing more.

2.

Treasures may come and treasures may go,
But memory lingers on.
And often in the box-room,
You are glad that they are gone.
A photograph, a manly calf,

Create a mild surprise,
A little hidden packet,
But who cares about the size?
For though hope eternal springs,
Life's made up of little things.

3.

Like the only piece of ermine in the family,
Respected and beloved by one and all.
It attained its quaintest shape
As a late Victorian cape,
When the Duchess was expecting . . . friends to call.
If the Bishop came to tea,
It was draped on the settee,
Till his lordship had an accident – a fall.
It was soft and warm and mellow,
Then it went a nasty yellow;
Still it's clothes that make the lady after all.

Refrain:

It's the only bit of fur left in the family,
No diary could describe its rise and fall.
Its career was somewhat marred,
By a queer young Coldstream Guard,
Who would wear it on his Bare Skin at a ball
It did see a bit of life,
On the squire's second wife;
Till it graced her husband's coffin as a pall.
Though it's worn by poor relations,
It has seen four coronations;
And it's clothes that make the lady after all.

Epilogue:

It has always been correct,
And will keep its self respect;
At the jumble sale to take its final call.
For in spite of family links,
We all know the damn thing stinks,
But it's clothes that make the lady after all.

Dougie had earned a vast amount of money during his long career and by the 1960s had spent most of it. He saved little but had always lived in great style, generously entertaining showbiz colleagues, friends and lovers. He gave large sums to charity (particularly theatrical ones) and was often a soft-touch for a true or false hard luck story. In 1964 he decided to move to Brighton and was offered a small, but very elegant, one bedroom Regency ground floor flat on Brighton's prestigious Arundel Terrace overlooking the seafront. His landlord, who lived upstairs, was the bisexual actor Robert Flemying who charged him six pounds a week rent, a sum that remained fixed until Dougie's death.

Brighton had long been established as a gay-friendly resort and in the early sixties also attracted a host of theatricals who made their home in the city. Laurence Olivier bought a house in Royal Crescent. His neighbours were John Clements and his actress wife Kay Hammond. Dora Bryan opened Clarges Hotel on the seafront. Flora Robson lived in an eccentric, gothic-like building in Wykeham Terrace. The French revue star Alice Delysia bought a flat in St George's Terrace. Terence Rattigan had a lavish home on the Marine Parade. Noel Coward, on his visits to England from his home in Jamaica, would make a point of seeing friends in Brighton. Everybody knew everybody and there were endless lunches and cocktail parties. Dougie fitted more than well into such a social atmosphere and, in 1969, after writing his autobiography, told his then agent, Dennis Van Thal of London Management, that he was retiring from the stage. It was a mistake – but one that was to be rectified in bizarre circumstances.

TOP: The legendary 1930s French Revue star Alice Delysia. She became a lifelong friend of Dougie and came to live near him in Brighton in the early 1960s.

R: Laurence Olivier, close neighbour and friend in Brighton during the 1960s and 70s

Bawdy but British!

PART TWO

5. THE LAST ACT

I rang the bell and the flat door opened, slowly and cautiously. A figure stood before me, majestic and comic, an elderly man wearing a bright green velvet suit and sporting a monocle. What was left of his receding hair was silvery, but had obviously been tinted blue and I could see faint traces of rouge blush on his white cheeks. His lips were glossed. He adjusted his monocle, peered at me, and suddenly beamed, offering me a hand that featured an enormous ring on it that resembled a heavily jewelled carbuncle. I wasn't sure whether to shake the hand or bow low and kiss it.

'Well, hello!' said the figure brightly. 'I'm Dougie Byng. Do come into my little abode, won't you? It's not much but I like to think of it as a last bastion of elegance in this depraved world of ours.'

The year was 1971. Dougie was 78 and I was 16. That year I had been working temporarily as an assistant in Better Books in Charing Cross Road saving up money to go to drama school. I wanted to be an actor. In Better Books I had discovered Dougie's autobiography and had written to him saying how much I had enjoyed it. I also told him I wanted to go into showbusiness. He had generously replied with a long letter written in lavish, almost antique, handwriting on gilt-edged paper. He suggested that should I ever visit Brighton then I should look him up for 'a spot of afternoon tea, nothing fancy you understand . . . '. I took the first train down to Brighton.

As he ushered me into his small front living room, with its large windows overlooking Brighton seafront, I was reminded for a moment of the interior of the Brighton Pavilion with its glorious Regency furniture, oil paintings and gilt. This was a mini-version of the Pavilion complete with tapestries and silks and silver-framed photographs of actresses and matinee idols long since dead.

Dougie gazed out of the window and then suddenly made a violent movement with his right arm which went crashing through the air like some triumphant footballer who had just scored a goal. This was the famous nervous twitch, which on first sight was alarming.

The twitch over he disappeared down a narrow hallway into a kitchen and reappeared moments later heavily pushing an enormous trolley laden with piles of neatly cut cucumber sandwiches, a choice of two large cakes together with two boiled eggs each. The teapot and cups were made of the finest porcelain and neatly starched napkins lay wrapped inside silver rings.

'You will take China, won't you?' he said, holding the teapot precariously and twitching violently at the same time. Drops sprayed onto the expensive carpet. 'And you must have an egg. I am a great believer in afternoon tea, aren't you ?' 'Indeed,' I replied, deeply impressed at this whole routine.

'You know, I'm a fossil from a bygone age,' he said cheerfully as he cracked an eggshell. 'And I'm so old that I have to go to the florist to get wired every month. I'm at the age when people come up to me in the street and ask, 'Weren't you Douglas Byng?' But I have no plans to return to the stage. I prefer my memories.'

This last line was said with no conviction whatsoever. You could tell he was champing at the bit to make a comeback. As the afternoon wore on, what amazed me was the sheer depth of his memory. He described a figure such as Sarah Bernhardt in such detail that he might well have seen her the day before. He had first spotted her as a young boy, being helped through the stage door of the London Coliseum.

'It was a shocking sight,' he said. 'There she was, dressed in white, and with only one leg. The other had been amputated. She was always trying to put on a brave face but you could see that her beauty was gone, there were lines of pain written all over her. I had to turn away.'

Spruced up at 70 years of age

As our tea party wore on (and it had all the atmosphere of a party) Dougie reminisced with ease about Noel Coward, New York speakeasies, London nightlife and much more. He was a born raconteur, the very best. When I left some hours later and walked along the seafront I was in some sort of trance, a heady glow, as if a part of me had found something I had wanted to or wished to be a part of. I had told Dougie that I was going to be an actor and he was encouraging.

As soon as I got back to London I wrote to every drama school in the book. Some months later I successfully auditioned for the London School of Dramatic Art. On my first day at school there was a telegram waiting for me. It read simply, 'To the start of something wonderful' and was signed 'Dougie'.

I started to visit Dougie regularly, usually every fortnight on the weekends, sometimes for a whole day and occasionally for the night. He bought me a camp bed to sleep in, delighting in the word 'camp', adding, 'I hope you don't think I'm being suggestive.' He wasn't. He was the perfect gentleman.

We would often go out to lunch at a nearby restaurant and before-hand he would spend what seemed like hours getting ready, fussing over a Hawes and Curtis suit ('I bought this in 1950 and it's still perfect'), choosing a silk tie or dabbing large amounts of Floris cologne all over his face. He would gaze into the bathroom mirror, pouting and twitching, sleeking back the dyed blue hair, muttering, 'In a previous life I think I must have been Mrs Fitz-herbert, mistress to the Prince Regent.'

The routine seemed to get longer and longer each time and one day I said impatiently, 'Oh, for God's sake, Dougie, we'll be here all day like this!'

He suddenly snapped back, 'Listen dearie, I never go outside my door unless I look like Douglas Byng.' I shut up.

Brighton was chock-a-block with parties in the seventies and Dougie positively revelled in them. He received two or three invitations a week which gave him ample chance to dress up and tell another fund of stories. The parties were either theatrical or gay and were often hosted by the discreet elderly queens who had made their home in the town after the Second World War. To the outside world (outside Brighton, that is) these queens seemed respectable but once indoors in those large, fading, dingy Regency houses, they became outrageous, blooming like rare orchids with their acid remarks and riotous memories.

It seemed to me then that there was hardly anyone at these parties under the age of 80 and the last time that any of them had been to the cinema, it was to see *Gone With The Wind* the first time round. Most of them were now single, their partners having died from either a heart attack or senility, and yet each of them was sexually rampant. Whenever Dougie took me along to one of these evenings I was both fascinated and yet filled with dread at the same time. I knew it would be impossible to have a sensible conversation with anyone without some old queen coming out with the line, 'I bet you've got a big one,' or with a sly wink ask, 'Do you go all the way?' It was a standard ritual. You blushed and tried to change the subject but you got absolutely nowhere. Before the evening was out you were told every piece of scandal that had happened in the town for the past fifty years and after your smeared sherry glass had been plied again with a refill for the sixth time, a discreet, gilt-edged card was slipped into your breast pocket with a telephone number on it. As you left the gathering a hand from nowhere would suddenly reach out and grasp you so hard it seemed impossible to think that it could belong to an 80-year-old, and you'd hear the words, 'Duckie, you know the moment I saw you, I knew we were going to be friends,' and as a mouth panting with hot, alcoholic breath came closer to your ear, you'd hear the words, 'Do call me.'

Dougie's own parties were of a different kind. They were not just held for pure entertainment but often to honour a friend if they had a birthday or happened to be in town. When the great musical comedy star Evelyn Laye was appearing at the Theatre Royal,

Dougie pulled all the stops out at his tiny flat. The place was crammed with theatricals – all drinking pink champagne. It was a noisy affair with guests clambering over each other, reaching for canapes and olives, while Dougie's arm flayed wildly as he nearly threw a tray of sausage rolls out of the window. A bewildered Evelyn Laye, then in her eighties, sat on the chaise longue, but managed a regal smile for everyone.

'Anyone for more champagne?,' Dougie cried loudly, 'There's plenty more for everyone! Just help yourselves!'

With Dougie there was never any expense spared despite the fact that he now had few funds in the bank. He had no respect for money. He thought it was for spending. At his local bistro he always insisted on paying the bill and if you offered to treat him, or pay half, a row would ensue. At one period he announced to all his friends that the cost of eating out was 'horrendous' and declared that he was going to economise. 'I'm going to start giving small, simple lunches at home,' he said.

The small, simple lunches turned into banquets involving four courses, a choice of wines, a table complete with candelabra and endless fetching and carrying from the kitchen. The sheer cost of the lunch was almost treble was it would have cost at the local bistro, but Dougie was in his element, fully dressed in red velvet suit with a silk cravat, and always holding court with a string of anecdotes. With the coffee and the brandy you often got the full rendering of one of his songs.

MILLIE THE MERMAID

A Lament

If all the fish the seas provide
Were placed together side by side
With wreckage washed up by the tide
You'd get a sketch of me.
Down in the depths where monsters leap,
Where giant crabs their vigil keep,

And rotting corpses come to sleep,
  I take my morning tea.
I was once famous, fresh and fair,
  The siren with the coral hair
  And every mariner's despair –
The man-trap of the sea.
  Ah! Well, those days have passed,
  I've lost my lure at last.

I'm Millie, a messy old mermaid,
Out and about all the day,
Combing my hair – what little is there –
  And just shouting my voice away.
  If I'm a bit thick and p'raps minus a fin,
  It's a din to suppose that I show it.
What a failure I've been in the last forty years,
  Every sailor I've seen must have wool in his ears,
If a whaler harpooned me I'd give him three cheers,
  Oh! I'm well on the rocks and I know it.

I'm Millie, a messy old mermaid,
Hanging out here on the line,
  Singing my song, I've been here so long,
I'm very near pickled with brine.
Oh, I know I've gone stale and my shape's like a whale,
And my tail has got bunions below it,
  When my throat went so dry shouting out 'Ship ahoys'
To a boat sailing by I just cried 'Hello boys!'
  But the only reply was a very rude noise.
Oh! I'm well on the rocks and I know it.

In the seventies Dougie's attitude towards homosexuality was a curious one. Gay liberation evolved in Britain in 1970 with the founding of the Gay Liberation Front (GLF). There were articles in newspapers and reports on television of the front's activities but Dougie wanted no involvement whatsoever with the idea of gay liberation or what it stood for. 'I don't know why people have to go round telling the world they are gay,' he remarked wearily to the writer Peter Burton.

Like his friend, 'the gorgeous Gael', the flamboyant Micheal MacLiammoir, who, when asked by a gay campaigner to participate in a march on the Irish government to make representations replied, 'My dear fellow, I will have nothing to do with it. They will only give us a bad name,' Dougie wished to be left alone with his own lifestyle. But he was not, and never had been, 'in the closet' and, surprisingly, always agreed to interviews or features in the up and coming gay press of the seventies. True, he gave little away about his private life, preferring to talk about the Cafe de Paris or pantomime, but he was prominently featured as a gay icon in such publications – and had no qualms about it.

Flamboyant Ango-Irish actor Micheal MacLiammoir: 'I will have nothing to do with Gay Liberation. It will only give us all a bad name . . .'

During that era I contributed to *Q International*, a gay glossy magazine, and did interviews with personalities such as the writer Robin Maugham and the ballet legend Anton Dolin. Dougie was my first feature in the magazine. Ironically, when I approached stars such as Ian McKellen and Derek Jacobi they politely refused interviews. Jacobi – who I knew briefly – sent me a note which read, 'I am so sorry but I don't at this stage have the same courage as the likes of Dougie Byng or Robin Maugham. Maybe I will one day.' Ian McKellen did not 'come out' until 1988 (a year after Dougie's death) and Jacobi only made his 27 year relationship with the actor Richard Clifford known publicly when the pair entered a civil partnership in 2006. In 1982, after making a guest appearance at a charity show at the gay Cricketer's Pub in Battersea, South London, Dougie' s photograph took up the whole of the front page of the newspaper *Capital Gay*. He was then 89 years old.

Every time Dougie rang me at my flat in London in the early seventies he sounded restless. I knew that he wanted to get back to work again and so one day I put his name forward as a possible guest for Michael Parkinson's TV chat show, then one of the most popular programmes on TV. A researcher was sent down to Brighton to check that Dougie wasn't senile and within a couple of weeks he was booked for the show. His co-stars for the show were Broadway legend Carol Channing and Irish wit Terry Wogan. Dougie proved to be the unexpected hit of the programme and I knew that this was the start of a new career for him. Douglas Byng – raconteur.

Songwriter and revue artiste Billy Milton. He and Dougie teamed up in the two hander revue, Those Thirties Memories, directed by Patrick Newley. Billy was then 83 and Dougie 93.

(photo: Colin Bourner)

6. CURTAIN CALLS

I became a sort of manager for him. I knew the kind of programmes he would be good on and soon more TV chat shows followed. He was also in demand to give talks to theatre groups. One day I got a telephone call from a lady in Bournemouth:

'We want a 1930s star to be in our forthcoming summer festival, can you supply one?'

'Douglas Byng,' I replied sharply.

'Who's he?' the lady asked.

'Look him up in *Who's Who in Theatre*,' I said. 'He's got three pages.'

The lady from Bournemouth phoned again the next day. 'I had no idea that Mr Byng was so famous,' she trilled. 'We'd like him for two weeks, twice daily.'

I nearly dropped the phone with shock. 'You do realise he's nearly 90?' I said.

'Will that be a problem?' came the reply.

'Well, er, not really,' I said gingerly, 'but he'll need someone to work with him. May I suggest the performer and pianist Billy Milton ?'

'Who's he ?'

'Look him up in *Who's Who in Theatre*. He's got three pages.'

Dougie was excited. So was Billy – and he was only 83. We all met up at the National Film Theatre cafe on the South Bank one lunchtime before taking a first class train to Bournemouth. Dougie arrived in a hired, chauffeur-driven car and Billy came on the bus. Each was dressed immaculately. Dougie had brought five suitcases and Billy a small shopping bag.

We had a splendid compartment, all to ourselves, on the train. Everything was perfect. It was then I discovered something about Dougie and Billy. They hated each other. And always had.

I was sitting next to Dougie who, by now, was beginning to go somewhat deaf. Billy sat facing us.

Dougie:'You know, dearie, (shouting at me) I'm very surprised they booked Billy – he was never a star. You don't mean he's going to do an act?'

Billy: (turning to me) 'I can't really bear the thought of two weeks with Dougie. You will keep him out of my way, won't you ?'

Dougie: 'Is he saying something about me, dearie? Tell him to speak up, will you ?'

Billy: 'If she goes on like this any longer, I'm getting off at the next stop.'

We arrived at Bournemouth and were greeted like visiting royalty by the theatre's management. Happiness prevailed until we were shown backstage to the dressing rooms. Dougie insisted on the number one and Billy ended up in the number two. Later that afternoon he placed a note on the door which read: 'Number One dressing room – Billy Milton.'

The show opened to a large audience which included the Mayor of Bournemouth and a gaggle of landladies. Billy played the piano to perfection, interspersing his own compositions with anecdotes about Noel Coward, Mistinguett and Maurice Chevalier. The audience loved him. But Dougie did not.

'Why on earth does he go on and on?' he asked me in the dressing room where he could hear the show on the Tannoy. 'I mean, are they really interested in all those old stories?'

When Dougie went on some of the audience gave him a standing ovation. He told some stories and gags and sang some of his best known songs. He overran his spot by fifteen minutes but the audience couldn't get enough of him. Except Billy.

'Why oh why does she go on and on?' he asked me in the dressing room. 'I mean who's interested in all those old stories?'

This went on for the whole two weeks, but worse still were the evenings when the fans came backstage clutching books and records to be signed. If there were more fans in Dougie's dressing room, there would be a loud shout from Billy: 'Why are people going in there? They've come to see me!' When an admirer went into Billy's dressing room, Dougie almost went white and shouted, 'He's gone to the wrong dressing room! Tell him I'm in here!'

The two rarely spoke off-stage despite staying in the same hotel and in rooms next to each other. The walls were paper thin so they could both hear each other's telephone conversations. 'You wouldn't think that Billy had any friends,' Dougie once remarked.

There was one exception to all this drama when, one Sunday, we were invited to tea by the management of the Royal Bath Hotel. The three of us sat in the sunshine in the hotel gardens drinking champagne at Dougie's insistence. There was no arguing and the two of then began to recall past glories. Eventually both of them nodded off and when the afternoon became chilly, Billy woke up, patted Dougie on the hand and said, 'Dougie, dear, we've a show to do tonight.'

Dougie stirred and muttered, 'Oh, I suppose we should be getting along, dearie.' They helped each other up and as they walked through the hotel, Dougie said to Billy, 'You know it's been a long time. We must be the oldest working performers in the business. No one can criticise us anymore.'

I teamed them together again on several occasions and once or twice the press got wind of their mutual animosity. *The Mail on Sunday* newspaper ran a spread on the two of them and captioned it 'Those Sunshine Boys' after the Neil Simon play in which two feuding vaudevillians team up together for one last show.

Dougie and Billy were oblivious to anything written about them because by then neither of them could hardly read a word. Both were almost blind as bats. In retrospect, it was slightly unfair of me to put them together on the same bill. Dougie was by far the bigger name and he was correct in saying that Billy had never been a star, but, nevertheless, in his thirties heyday, Billy was a headliner of sorts. He had made a series of frothy British musical films and mixed with the good and great. Unlike Dougie, who had long been careful about his reputation and private life, Billy positively flaunted his homosexuality and had done so for years. Some people said that this had hampered his career.

'Those Sunshine Boys' ~ Billie Milton and Dougie backstage at the London Palladium

Bawdy but British!

I produced a short documentary film about the two of them which we shot one afternoon in the number one dressing room at the London Palladium. There was no script and the three of us just sat there talking while the director, Ken Butler (an ex protégé of Derek Jarman) let the cameras roll. The theatre critic Jack Tinker had heard we were in the theatre and came round to see us. The next thing he was in the film.

Later there were more stage shows and neither Dougie or Billy showed any signs of flagging. Each show was completely different and largely depended on what mood either of them was in.

Off-stage Billy was a waspish individual who, unlike Dougie, had few real friends. He lived in a tiny flat in Kensington High Street above a halal butchers, for which he paid a minimal rent, although the landlord was always trying to evict him on account of his piano playing all day. The piano, a baby grand, took up almost the entire floor of the flat. Billy claimed that it was a present from Cole Porter. He said he'd slept with Cole – but then Billy always claimed he'd slept with everyone.

On the days I used to visit him for lunch he was a kind and witty host with a fund of stories about his early days in Hollywood. Over cheese and sandwiches and glasses of scotch I would listen to his tales about his stay at the famous Garden of Allah where he had wined and dined with W C Fields and Tallulah Bankhead. Yet somehow every story seem to end up as a wild, sexual scandal and in most cases included violent scenes of flagellation. Even at the age of 83, Billy could get very worked up and excited when talking and his face would flush bright red as his stories got more lurid.

'Errol Flynn! Now what about him?' he would gasp. 'He loved to be furiously whipped! Yes, whipped, my dear!'. He spat the words out and seemed almost shocked as he rested his head back in his chair, as if telling the tale had exhausted him. There was more.

'Flo Ziegfeld. Awful man! Awful! You know he liked a golden shower? You would walk backstage and see some dancer with her tights off pissing all over him. Monstrous! Absolutely monstrous!'

I listened to these tales regularly, not always believing them, but I was always in awe of their rich perversity and the sheer energy with which Billy told them. Everything for Billy was a performance. He was totally alive.

I also had to admire his independence and lifestyle. He had virtually no money and was a proud man, who, when not performing, spent most of his time alone composing songs – he'd written over 200 – or going to the cinema. He was a jaunty figure who was a familiar sight in Kensington High Street, sauntering along with a spring in his step, as he went shopping every morning. 'Steady the Buffs,' he would say if you were walking with him and sometimes he would add, 'Everything points to happiness.' I once asked him where that phrase had come from. 'My father used to say that when the bailiffs came around to collect our furniture,' he said. 'Everything points to happiness.'

If Billy could be anti-social then Dougie was the opposite and even in his nineties was still entertaining at his flat in Brighton. But not all social occasions went to plan. In 1983, I was, for a brief period, Quentin Crisp's manager and press agent while he was appearing in his one man show in the West End and later on tour. I had known Quentin on and off for about five years and had become one of his 'little helpers'. Quentin was hopeless at doing everyday tasks and famously admitted that the only ambition he had as a child was to be a chronic invalid.

One Sunday be was booked to appear at Hove Town Hall and I decided to take him along beforehand to have tea with Dougie. The two had never met.

We arrived on Dougie's doorstep. Quentin was wearing a black velvet suit, a fedora hat, blue rinsed hair and full make-up complete with mascara. He looked like an elderly Dusty Springfield. The door opened and there was Dougie in a green velvet suit, mauve rinsed hair, rouged cheeks with traces of powder and a hint of mascara on his lips. He looked like Dame Gladys Cooper.

Bawdy but British!

'How kind of you to have made the effort to come,' said Dougie testily as he ushered us in.

'Oh, I think making any sort of effort in one's life is a mistake,' said Quentin in his best nasal tones as he glided through the doorway.

Dougie looked at me, tut tutted, and said, 'Peculiar, most peculiar.'

Tea was served with scones, cream and jam. Quentin tucked into them as if he hadn't eaten for a week. Dougie gave a violent twitch and a scone fell to the floor.

'This is very cosy,' said Quentin, looking round the room.

'Quentin's doing a one-man show at Hove Town Hall,' I said, trying to break the ice between them.

'Really?' said Dougie sharply. 'It's a terrible place. I wouldn't be seen dead playing there.'

'Oh, I go where I'm told,' said Quentin, lowering his eyes to the floor. 'I don't make decisions. They make them for me. I am an existentialist. You learn to swim with the tide – but faster.'

The self-styled 'stately homo of England' Quentin Crisp. He and Dougie did not hit it off when they met.

'Extraordinary,' said Dougie, turning to me. 'What on earth's he talking about ? Who's an existentialist? I don't know what's going on at all.'

I realised, then and there, that the idea of these two men meeting together under the same roof was a gigantic mistake. I should have known. Both were dazzlingly egocentrical, at times like haughty peacocks, and whilst Quentin was normally noted for his almost saint-like tolerance of other people, on this occasion his patience was sorely tested. Dougie, who wasn't working, was incensed that another person, who not only looked like himself, but was also more than a match in wit and style, should be appearing in a one-man show literally down the road. I racked my brains for a solution to the embarrassing situation but both of them solved it instantly. They decided to talk at the same time – and completely ignore each other.

Dougie got up, stood at the window, and began: 'When I starred at the Cafe de Paris in the 1930s people actually fought to get tickets . . . '.

Quentin, remaining seated with teacup in hand said: 'It was Miss Garbo who fornicated liberally, but with immense taste and . . .' This astonishing routine performed by the two of them lasted nearly half an hour and would easily have provided Samuel Beckett with enough material for a full play and it could have continued forever had I not suggested to Quentin that it was time to leave for Hove Town Hall. Both of them, by now somewhat hoarse from their non-stop monologues, seemed hugely relieved. As I showed Quentin to the doorway Dougie glared at me and said nothing. I knew Quentin wouldn't be visiting again.

The next day I rang my friend Peter Burton, who knew both of them well, and told him of the previous day's events. He said to me, 'Putting those two old queens together in one room?

You must have been crackers.' Quite.

Throughout his long life Dougie had never had a permanent partner. Indeed, it is difficult to imagine anyone sharing his virtual non-stop showbusiness life. Like Sir John Gielgud, he was remarkably unworldly and knew nothing about current affairs or everyday life. He read the *Daily Telegraph* – but purely for the theatre reviews or fashion pages. Nothing existed outside of the theatre.

No partner could have put up with his fastidious habits off-stage and in his elegant Brighton flat he liked everything to be in its place. There was no cleaner or maid to dust the many silver-framed portraits of friends or to Hoover the Persian carpets. He insisted on doing everything himself.

He and I were never lovers although love existed in our relationship in a platonic, caring way. When I first met him I was the young fan and he was flattered at my interest. He was also protective of me. As I grew older, and then became his manager, our relationship changed and we were on almost equal footing. We even argued about theatre. Then, as he grew older still and more infirm, the relationship altered again and I became protective, fiercely so, of him. We often walked arm-in-arm along Brighton seafront together. Mind you, if we hadn't – he would have been blown away.

We did one last show in Brighton in 1986 with Billy Milton. Peter Burton was in the audience: 'It opened with an ovation which continued ringing round the theatre well after Dougie had left the stage,' he said. 'Though infirm – he was seated for most of the evening – Dougie knew how to captivate an audience until the very end. His was a very long run indeed – rather like Sheila Van Damm's Windmill – the Dougie Byng show never really closed.'

Comedian Roy Hudd was also there: 'It was a marvellous evening. I remember in reply to one query, 'Did you ever see Lady Beerbohm Tree? Dougie replied, 'Yes, I saw her once at a charity matinee.

She walked on in a purple crinoline with purple ostrich feathers, a purple fan and elbow-length gloves, and wearing a diamond necklace, tiara and bracelet. She picked up a kitchen chair, put it downstage, sat on it and said to the audience, 'Now I want you all to imagine I'm a plumber's mate!'

'He also talked about being banned by the BBC for being too blue. He told a story about two matronly ladies visiting a friend. Once inside their friend's house they heard, through an open kitchen door, the end of a children's programme about bird life. Alas they only caught the back announcement as the presenter said, 'So remember, children – tits like coconuts.' 'Oh!' cried one, 'Turn that wireless off! They're listening to that dreadful Douglas Byng.'

His very last professional appearance was a special one. I managed to get him a booking for one night at the National Theatre where he appeared in the Cottesloe Studio. It was December 1986 and the management thought that as Christmas was approaching, Dougie was a theatrical figure that was most synonymous with the spirit of pantomime, even though his days of dressing up were long over.

In a simple velvet suit and with a minimum of stage make-up he held a full house captive for over an hour. A stage hand offered him the use of a microphone but he politely refused it much to the delight of the audience. 'I've been on stage for nearly eighty years now and I've never used one yet,' he said. I stood in the wings and murmured, 'Eighty years . . . '. It had to be a record.

I listened to all the familiar stories, Mrs Patrick Campbell, the Cochran revues, New York, Noel Coward, Cole Porter – the list went on like a personal history of the theatre. He sang *I'm a Tree* and *Miss Otis Regrets* and at the end of the show the audience, a mixture of old and young alike, gave him a warm and spontaneous standing ovation. As he came offstage he looked at me earnestly and said, 'Did I do alright, dearie?' His face was flushed red and he had all the eagerness of a twelve-year-old boy appearing in his first school play. 'Yes, Dougie, ' I replied. 'You really did.'

Although his memory was as alert as ever his general health was failing and he was unable to look after himself on his own in Brighton. I travelled backwards and forward from London to see him as often as I could and his landlord, Robert Flemying, kept and eye on him but neither of us could be with Dougie 24 hours a day. He needed round-the-clock nursing. It was reluctantly agreed by all his friends that he should be admitted to Denville Hall, the actors' retirement home in Middlesex. Dougie protested wildly at the idea and it was a sad day for his friends when he had to leave Brighton, the town he had called 'both breezy and salty.'

In Denville Hall he proved to be the resident from hell, describing the place as ' a bad dream, dearie, I'm hoping at any moment to wake up in my own bed in Brighton. I hate this fucking place, for one thing everyone is so fucking old.'

Stage and screen star Robert Flemyng who was Dougie's landlord in Brighton for many years.

(photo: Colin Bourner)

He cursed and swore at the ever patient and caring nurses who pretended they hadn't heard him and he told the doctors that all he wanted to do was to 'die quickly' although in reality he was afraid of death. It was the last thing he wanted. Friends, like Richard Attenborough and Barry Cryer, dropped in to see him regularly and I visited him as much as I could.

One afternoon he was lying half-asleep in bed mumbling to himself. I sat on the edge of the bed and squeezed his hand. 'Oh, it's you, dearie,' he said brusquely. 'You know this is all down to the Devil? He's come to collect.'

I hadn't the faintest idea what he was talking about and presumed the nurses had put him on some medication. 'The Devil? What's all that about?' I asked.

'Well, it's like this,' he said staring blankly at the ceiling. 'The Devil came to me when I was a young man and told me that I could have this fabulous career, I would be hugely wealthy and have my name in lights and never be out of work. My career would last for years – but there was a price. I would have a hideous old age and a terrible end in pain.'

'Rubbish,' I said. 'You're just making that up. There's not a word of truth in it.'

He gave a deep sigh. 'Well, it's almost the truth.'

On the morning of August 24 1987 he slipped into a coma and died. He was 94.

David Raven (drag artiste Maisie Trollette) and Dougie pictured backstage after Dougie's penultimate performance, Brighton, 1987

Bawdy but British!

His obituaries in the broadsheet newspapers were lengthy. *The Daily Telegraph* described him as 'one of the most redoubtable entertainers of the 20th century . . . his achievements as an artiste in revue, variety, cabaret and indeed pantomime were legendary. He was accorded the sobriquet of 'High Priest of Camp' long before the theatrical word 'camp' became part of common usage.' The Times dubbed him 'a dazzling performer, a theatrical legend.'

He was cremated without any religious service or mourners, as strictly specified in his will ('I want people to remember me from a box in the theatre, not a box at a funeral') and his ashes were scattered by his old friend Eric Payne over the colourful gardens that lay outside his flat on Brighton's seafront. Characteristically he had composed his own epitaph:

So here you are, old Douglas, a derelict at last,
Before your eyes, what visions rise of your vermilion past.
Mad revelry beneath the stars, hot clasping by the lake.
You need not sigh, you can't deny, you've had your bit of cake.

Still looking dapper ~
Dougie at 90

Old Father
Thames
~ Firth
Shepherd
revue

Bawdy but British!

AFTERWORD

One morning I was sitting in Dougie's living room drinking a cup of coffee. I had stayed the night and Dougie was in the bathroom having a shave. I gazed out of the window and saw shafts of early morning sunlight glisten on the sea. Fishing boats bobbed up and down. Then I looked around the room, saw the oil paintings on the wall, the antique furniture, the framed pictures of Dougie's showbusiness friends and the pile of scrapbooks neatly stacked on a marble-topped table. A grandfather clock in the hallway struck eight.

Quite suddenly, and for no reason at all, I realised that one day all this would be gone. Furniture, scrapbooks, Dougie Byng himself. None of it would exist anymore, this way of life, a culture, civilised and elegant, it would be nothing more than a memory.

I looked out again at the sea and felt rather sad.

At that moment Dougie appeared in the room. 'Well, what shall we do today, dearie?' he asked. Before I could answer he said, 'I know, let's dress up and I'll take you to lunch. I'll order oysters and we must drink pink champagne.' And with that he gave a big smile.

BIBLIOGRAPHY

BAKER, Roger	*Drag* (Triton Books 1968)
BOURNE, Stephen	*Brief Encounters* (Cassell 1996)
BOURNE, Stephen	*Elisabeth Welch* (Scarecrow Press 2005)
BYNG, Douglas	*As You Were* (Duckworth 1970)
BYNG, Douglas	*Byng Ballads* (Bodley Head 1933)
BYNG Douglas	*More Byng Ballads* (Bodley Head 1935)
FAWKES, Richard	*Fighting for a Laugh* (Macdonald and Janes, 1978)
GUINNESS, Alec	*Blessings In Disguise* (Hamish Hamilton 1985)
MILLER, Neil	*Out of the Past* (Vintage 1995)
NEWLEY, Patrick	*The Amazing Mrs Shufflewick* (Third Age Press, 2007)
NEWLEY, Patrick	*The Krays and Bette Davis* (Authors Online 2005)
NEWLEY, Patrick	*You Lucky People! – The Tommy Trinder Story* (Third Age Press, 2008)

SELECT RECORDINGS

There are numerous 78s of Douglas Byng's songs which are collectors items. Many of them, however, can be heard on the excellent compilation CD, *Naughty Nights with Douglas Byng*, which is released on the Flapper Label (Pavilion Records). The CD has an excellent biographical note by Tony Barker. Available from music shops or on Amazon.co.uk

Douglas Byng Looks Back is an LP that was released on the Decca Ace of Clubs Label in 1970. This contains 14 songs which Byng recorded especially for the album. The accompaniment was directed by Eric Rogers and piano accompaniment is by Alan Leigh. The LP was produced by Raymond Ware. This LP is long out of print.

ACKNOWLEDGEMENTS

I should like to thank the following for their help with this book: Richard Anthony Baker, The late Frith Banbury, Colin Bourner, Peter Burton, Roy Hudd, Eric Midwinter, Lynette Ray, Nina Saunders, Michael Thornton and the late Jack Tripp.

INDEX

RAVES & REVIEWS
about 'Mrs Shufflewick' & Tommy Trinder

Deeply enjoyable. Patrick Newley has done us all a great favour by producing this admirably succinct memoir, with its rare photographs, outrageous anecdotes, transcribed routines and perceptive affection. SIMON CALLOW, The Guardian

Patrick Newley has written a smashing biography of Rex, The Amazing Mrs Shufflewick. It is a little masterpiece. ROY HUDD, Yours Magazine.

Unforgettable. This biography with all the laughter and desperation is a must for the bookshelf of every entertainment afficianado. WYN CALVIN

A truly wonderful book. BARRY CRYER

I loved it! VICTOR SPINETTI

Newley interweaves the text with extracts from Shuff's scripts which are so skillfully written that one can imagine how Jameson played them and get a real flavour of what meeting Mrs Shufflewick was really like. For those who saw Mrs S live, this is a wonderful reminder of that talent and a fitting tribute clearly written with great affection. TOM HOWARD, Rogues and Vagabonds

Patrick Newley's new biography of **Tommy Trinder** *is a slim volume, but it is the equal of any fat tome, since Newley tells his story with the same sort of machine-gun delivery as Trinder worked his act.* RICHARD ANTHONY BAKER, The Stage.

A top notch tale, full of rich pickings, but always keeping up a lively pace and never losing its compact structure. Tommy Trinder is himself one of those lucky people. His life story has been superbly told by Patrick Newley. ERIC MIDWINTER

Masterly and witty. It gives a very vivid picture of what Tommy Trinder must have been like. JONATHAN CECIL

If you liked *BAWDY BUT BRITISH!*

~you'll love ...

THE AMAZING MRS SHUFFLEWICK
The Life of Rex Jameson

also by Patrick Newley
£12.50 paperback + 15% postage
120 pages
ISBN 1898576 21 1

Illustrated with photographs and playbills

'Weak willed and easily lead', Mrs Shufflewick was a rednosed, drunken old cockney who liked nothing better than to prop up the bar of her local while sipping large gin and tonics, Guinness, port and lemon or anything else that came to hand. She would tell outrageous stories about her private life to anyone who cared to listen and invariably, at the end of a disastrously alcoholic evening, would end up stark naked — all but her hairnet — on top of a 29 bus.

In real life Mrs Shufflewick was the glorious creation of Rex Jameson, a music hall great and one of radio and TV's most original and brilliant comics. Shy, difficult, bisexual and alcoholic, his private and public life often reached spectacular highs and appalling lows.

In this candid and incisive biography, Patrick Newley, who managed Jameson's later career, examines the life of the man who was lionised by comedians such as Bob Monkhouse, Barry Cryer, Danny La Rue and Barry Humphries. '*Rex was a comic genius,*' said Roy Hudd. '*Even in his cups he was gloriously funny.*'

YOU LUCKY PEOPLE!
The Tommy Trinder Story
by Patrick Newley
£12.50 paperback + 15% postage
130 pages
ISBN 1898576 23 8
Illustrated with
photographs and playbills
Published Sept 1, 2008

Tommy Trinder was one of Britain's greatest comics, an aggressive, working class performer who was regarded by many as the greatest ad-libber in showbusiness. His catchphrases 'You Lucky People!' and 'If it's laughter you're after, Trinder's the name!' became famous nationwide and his act, filled with insult and sexual innuendo, was rarely scripted.

He was a pioneer of live television stand-up comedy and, at the height of his fame in the 1940s and 50s, enjoyed superstar status, a rarity for any comedian then or since. He reigned supreme at the London Palladium, starred in a series of classic wartime films, became chairman of Fulham Football Club, and toured worldwide with his own shows.

Yet despite his charm and immense popularity, Tommy Trinder remained an enigma. Fiercely egocentrical and a notorious womaniser, he frequently clashed with his co-stars, both onstage and off, and at the very peak of his fame was sensationally axed as host from TV's *Sunday Night at the London Palladium*. Embittered but undeterred, he maintained a punishing work schedule until his death at the age of 80 in 1989.

MORE theatrical memorabilia . . .
I Say, I Say, I Say
The Double Act Story
by Eric Midwinter

£9.50 paperback + 15% postage
154 pages
ISBN 9781898576 28 0
Illustrated with
photographs and playbills
Published June 1, 2009

In this compact and original study of British comic double acts, Eric Midwinter cheerfully attempts to answer three questions.

FIRST, while describing the birth of the modern double act among the minstrel shows at late Victorian seaside, he wonders why there were so few double acts before 1918.

SECOND he asks why, then, was there such a profusion of double acts between 1920 and the mid'50s. He shows how the dictates of fashion, coupled with the demands of variety and 'wireless', created a boom time for the crosstalk comics.

THIRD, why, since that point, and with the intriguing exception of Morecambe and Wise, have there been so few comic duos. He analyses the effects of television and other social dimensions on popular entertainment by way of explanation.

Throughout there are brief and telling glimpses of scores of double acts, including some American examples, together with in-depth scrutiny of the more famous 'turns', and all related vividly to the social background of their audiences.

At once knowledgeable and readable, *I Say, I Say, I Say* is an attractively presented account of a measurable and significant element of popular entertainment over the last hundred or so years. Everyone has enjoyed a double act – the appeal of *I Say, I Say, I Say* is very general indeed.

Other Third Age Press books
by Eric Midwinter

As one *stage* door closes . . . The story of John Wade: Jobbing Conjuror

As one stage door closes . . . is a study of the way the entertainment world has changed over the past 50 years by shifts in the social and economic fabric, as personally witnessed by John Wade, who, over that period, has successfully plied the ancient craft of magicianship in every possible show-business outlet. In the course of his personal journey, he crosses paths with a sparkling array of stars. This book contrives to look both in front of and behind the scenes – and then locates both in social context. From the dingy theatrical lodgings and dreary train journeys of the 1950s to the sumptuous environs of luxury liners and Hollywood glamour 40 years on, this show-business saga unrolls. **176 pages £12.50 + 15% postage**

Novel Approaches: a guide to the popular classic novel

Oh for a good read and an un-putdownable book! Despite the lurid blandishments of television, there are still many of us who turn, quietly, pensively, to the novel in leisure moments. This short text is aimed at such people whose interest has been kindled sufficiently to permit some extra contemplation and study.

Novel Approaches takes 35 novels that have stood the test of time and embeds them in historical and literary commentary – a combination of social background giving scientific objectivity, and the author's artistic subjectivity.

180 pages £9.50 + 15% postage

THIRD AGE PRESS

... an independent publishing company which recognizes that the period of life after full-time employment and family responsibility can be a time of fulfilment and continuing development ... a time of regeneration.

 *. . . is a series (by Eric Midwinter) that focuses on the presentation of your unique life. These booklets* seek to stimulate and guide your thoughts and words in what is acknowledged to be not only a process of value to future generations but also a personally beneficial exercise.

A Voyage of Rediscovery: a guide to writing your life story
is a 'sea chart' to guide your reminiscence & provide practical advice about the business of writing or recording your story. **36 pages** **£4.50**

Encore: a guide to planning a celebration of your life
An unusual and useful booklet that encourages you to think about the ways you would like to be remembered, hopefully in the distant future. **20 pages** **£2.00**

The Rhubarb People ... Eric Midwinter's own witty and poignant story of growing up in Manchester in the 1930s. Also on tape including useful tips on writing or recording your story.
32 pages **£4.50** **audio cassette** **£5.00**

OR all 3 booklets for only £10 + 15% postage

Defining Women
. . . on mature reflection

£12.50+ 15% postage

160 pages

Edited by Dianne Norton
illustrated by Mig

The 'extraordinary ordinary women' invited to contribute to this anthology rose magnificently to the occasion, delving deep into their personal experiences and laying bare their innermost feelings as they met a variety of challenges. Gwen Parrish, U3A News

How to be a Merry Widow
~ life after death for the older lady

by Mary Rogers
Illustrated by Mig
£12.50 + 15% postage
166 pages

• *If you are looking for a politically correct, objective view of how to cope with bereavement – do NOT buy this book!*
• *This is a book about coming to terms with widowhood*
after the shock of bereavement has begun to ease.
• *Mary Rogers writes with candour and humour, in a deeply personal style. She manages to be funny, moving and at the same time, practical.*